Mel Bay Presents

Drum Lessons for Kids of All Ages

by Rob Silverman & Mike Silverman

CD CONTENTS

1	Clearwater (With Drums) [2:43]	9	Musical Mike's Theme (With Drums) [2:58]
2	Clearwater (Without Drums) [2:46]	10	Musical Mike's Theme (Without Drums) [2:57]
3	Jay's Room (With Drums) [3:04]	11	Rockin' Rob's Rock Song (With Drums) [2:11]
4	Jay's Room (Without Drums) [3:04]	12	Rockin' Rob's Rock Song (Without Drums) [2:12]
5	Tennessee (With Drums) [2:17]	13	The Drumming Blues (With Drums) [2:03]
6	Tennessee (Without Drums) [2:17]	14	The Drumming Blues (Without Drums) [2:02]
7	Mikey G (With Drums) [3:22]	15	One Fine Day (With Drums) [3:14]
8	Mikey G (Without Drums) [3:28]	16	One Fine Day (Without Drums) [3:10]

Graphic Layout by Rob Silverman

The playalong recording features:
Rob Silverman - Drums
Mike Silverman - Synthesizers
Chris Quest - Electric Bass

Visit us on the Web at www.melbay.com — E-mail us at email@melbay.com

Acknowledgments

I would like to thank the following people for their help and encouragement: Bobby Silverman, Fred Pierce, Andy Marks, Kevin Gianino, Zach Morrow, Adomi Gordon, Noel Neuenkirk, Joe Laycock, Steve Treder, Chad Smith, Daryl Whited, Casey "The Caveman" Adams, Derek Lauer, Larry Kornfeld, Sheldon Russell, Chris McCollum, Chris Condon, Mark Robertson, Rick Robertson, Chris Madalena, Kathy Silverman, Turtle, Mike King at Delta Springs, Steve Marshall at Cattle Productions, Bob Luther, John Kasica, Tom Stubbs, Kim Shelly, Hal Brigham, Paula Mass, Danny Theodoro, Andrew Cohen, Jason Rakers, Steve Missler, Gus Nanos, Steve Strayhorn, Harold and Peggy Rosenthal, Jay Stewart, my Mom and Dad.

I'd especially like to thank all of my young students that helped in the formation of this book.

Bob Silverman

4-19-00

Contents

Foreword

To The Teacher

This book is intended for the beginning drum student and includes many of the essential reading and playing skills for the snare and drumset. As a student and teacher of drums for more than twenty years, I saw a need for a fun book like this and set forth to create one. The snare drum and drumset studies are integrated in a logical, sequential order. For example, a new rhythm is introduced and studied on the snare drum and then applied to the drumset as a beat and then a fill. The same rhythm will appear later in the book for review and then in one of the playalong songs. This way, each concept is reinforced and used in different ways. The student will see progress and be inspired to continue to study reading music.

I have included dynamic markings in many of the snare drum exercises. I think it is necessary to stress the importance of dynamics right away and explain that a piece is not played correctly unless all of the dynamics are observed. The earlier the student becomes sensitive to dynamic changes, the better.

Cartoons and games have been included to help focus student interest.

To The Student

You may use this book as a self study method. But remember, nothing can replace the guidance of an experienced teacher. If you do not have one, I would suggest seeking one out. A good way to find one is to ask other drum students about their teachers. Find out about their methods and backgrounds. A teacher should be inspiring as a mentor.

Although this book is wacky and humorous, it contains the fundamental tools you will need to be a good drummer. Practice these skills consistently and you will see yourself improve.

Hi, I'm Rockin' Rob. I will be your host as you travel through this book of drum lessons! You will meet lots of my friends and learn how to play the drums.

Introducing Musical Mike

Hey Abe, show them the proper playing position.

OK, Rockin' Rob. How's this?

Great!

These are the parts of the snare drum and stand.

Snare throw off lever

Top hoop

Batter head

Lug casing

Tension rod

Bottom hoop

Damper adjustment screw

Shell

Angle adjustment screw

Height adjustment screw

Tripod

Snare but end

Try hitting the drum over and over with each hand.

OK!

This is a music staff. It has five lines with four spaces in between. Remember this page because we will see all of these later in the book!

Fifth Line

Fourth Space

Fourth Line

Third Space   Snare Drum Space!

Third Line

Second Space

Second Line

First Space

First Line

This is a quarter note. When you see a note, it means hit the drum.

This line is called the stem.

The egg shaped part is called the note head.

From here to here is called a measure.

This is called a barline. It separates the measures.

This is a percussion clef. It tells you that this is drum music.

The Double Stroke Roll

Why, Rockin' Rob?

One of the most important exercises for the hand is the double stroke roll!

Because many other rudiments are made from the double stroke roll! Also it sounds great on the drums!

R is for right hand and L is for left hand.
Hit the drum twice with each hand over and over.

R   R   L   L   L   R   R   R   L   L

Practice the double stroke roll
every day for five minutes.

First Snare Song

This is a time signature. It tells you how to count the beat. The top number tells you how many beats are in each measure. In this song there are four beats in each measure.

The bottom number tells you what kind of note receives the beat. In this song there are four quarter notes in each measure. Play the whole song below and count out loud.

f This is a musical symbol called **Forte**. It means to play with a full volume.

This is a quarter note. It means to hit the drum once!

This is a quarter rest. It means to count one beat of silence.

Largo (very slowly)

Hit 1   Hit 2   Hit 3   Hit 4   Don't Hit! 1   Don't Hit! 2   Don't Hit! 3   Don't Hit! 4

Hit 1   Don't Hit! 2   Hit 3   Don't Hit! 4   Hit 1   Hit 2   Don't Hit! 3   Don't Hit! 4

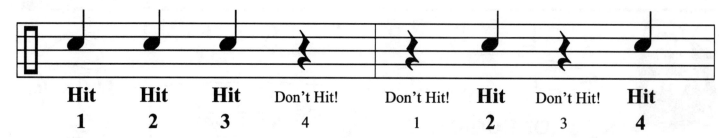

Hit 1   Hit 2   Hit 3   Don't Hit! 4   Don't Hit! 1   Hit 2   Don't Hit! 3   Hit 4

This is a double barline. It indicates the end of the song.

Hit 1   Hit 2   Don't Hit! 3   Hit 4   Don't Hit! 1   Hit 2   Hit 3   Don't Hit! 4

Counting Fun

Here is a fun way to count quarter notes and quarter rests.
Say "walk" for each quarter note and "rest" for each rest.

Largo

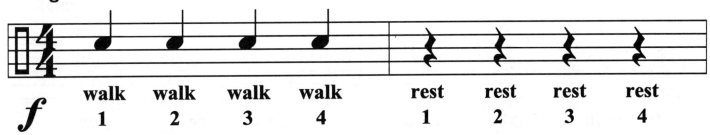

𝆑

walk	walk	walk	walk	rest	rest	rest	rest
1	2	3	4	1	2	3	4

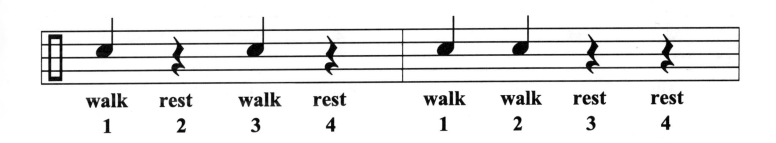

walk	rest	walk	rest	walk	walk	rest	rest
1	2	3	4	1	2	3	4

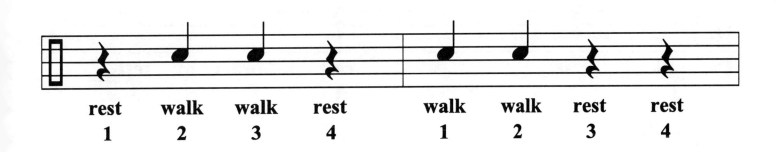

rest	walk	walk	rest	walk	walk	rest	rest
1	2	3	4	1	2	3	4

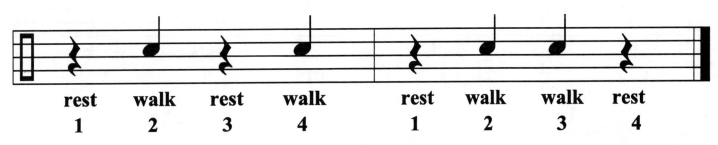

rest	walk	rest	walk	rest	walk	walk	rest
1	2	3	4	1	2	3	4

Let's Play Three Four Time

3 The top number is three. It tells you that there are three beats in each measure.

4 The bottom line is four. The quarter note receives the beat. There are three quarter notes in each measure.

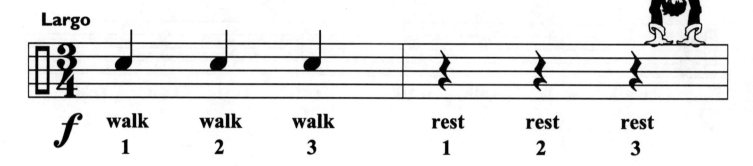

Largo

walk	walk	walk	rest	rest	rest
1	2	3	1	2	3

f

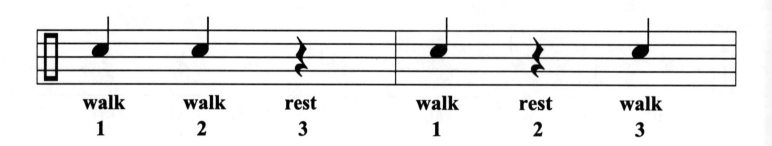

walk	walk	rest	walk	rest	walk
1	2	3	1	2	3

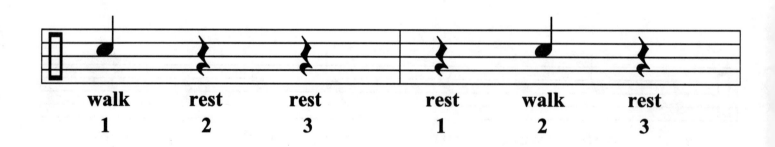

walk	rest	rest	rest	walk	rest
1	2	3	1	2	3

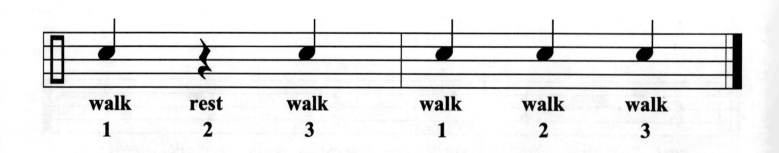

walk	rest	walk	walk	walk	walk
1	2	3	1	2	3

Half Notes are Fun!

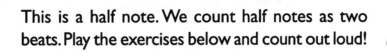 This is a half note. We count half notes as two beats. Play the exercises below and count out loud!

Largo

1

f   1   2   3   4

half   note   half   note

2

1   2   3   4

walk   walk   half   note

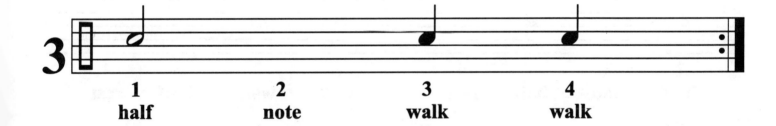

3

1   2   3   4

half   note   walk   walk

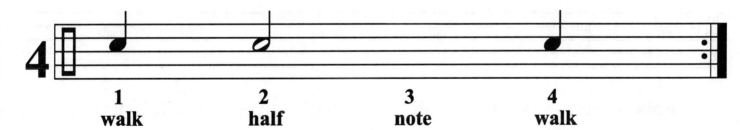

4

1   2   3   4

walk   half   note   walk

o This is a whole note. We count whole notes as four beats.

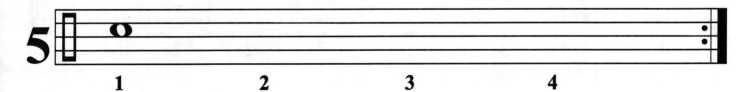

5

1   2   3   4

Introducing the Half Rest

This is a half rest. When you see this,
count two beats of silence.

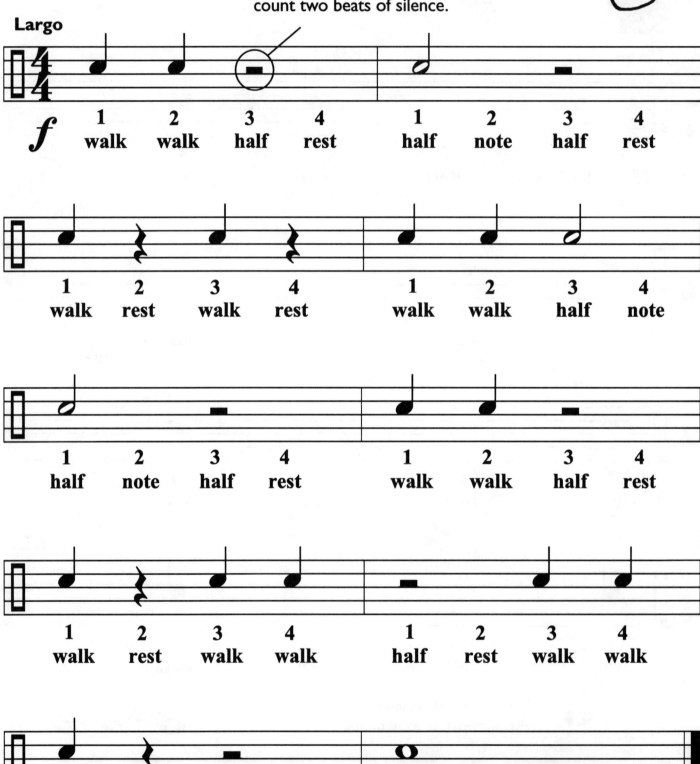

Largo

1	2	3	4	1	2	3	4
walk	walk	half	rest	half	note	half	rest

1	2	3	4	1	2	3	4
walk	rest	walk	rest	walk	walk	half	note

1	2	3	4	1	2	3	4
half	note	half	rest	walk	walk	half	rest

1	2	3	4	1	2	3	4
walk	rest	walk	walk	half	rest	walk	walk

1	2	3	4	1	2	3	4
walk	rest	half	rest				

16

Let's Learn our Eighth Notes

These are eighth notes. They are played twice as fast as quarter notes. When you count out loud, say "run-ning" for the eighth notes and "walk" for the quarter notes.

walk   run ning walk   walk   walk   run ning walk   walk

f Means **Forte**. Play at a loud volume.

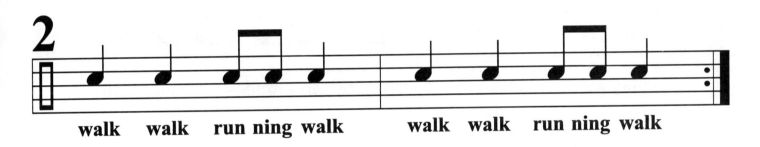

walk   walk   run ning walk   walk   walk   run ning walk

run ning walk   walk   walk   run ning walk   walk   walk

run ning run ning walk   walk   run ning run ning walk   walk

More Eighth Notes

The Eighth Note March

Each measure is a little different, so read the music carefully.
Count the rhythms both of the ways we have learned.

Tempo di marcia (March Tempo)

f

1	2	and	3	4	1	and	2	3	4
walk	run	ning	walk	walk	run	ning	walk	walk	walk

1	and	2	and	3	4	1	2	and	3	and	4	and
run	ning	run	ning	walk	walk	walk	run	ning	run	ning	run	ning

1	2	and	3	4	1	and	2	and	3	4
walk	run	ning	walk	walk	run	ning	run	ning	walk	walk

1	and	2	3	and	4	1	and	2	and	3
run	ning	walk	run	ning	walk	run	ning	run	ning	walk

19

Eighth Notes in Three Four

This song is in three four time. Remember that there are three beats in each measure.
Try counting this page using "walk, running" and then "one, and, two, and, three, and."

run ning run ning run ning   run ning walk walk
1 + 2 + 3 +   1 + 2 3

"+" means "and"

walk walk run ning   walk run ning run ning
1 2 3 +   1 2 + 3 +

walk walk run ning   run ning walk walk
1 2 3 +   1 + 2 3

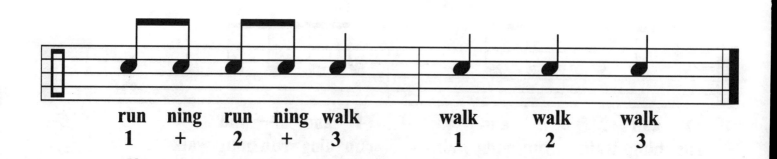

run ning run ning walk   walk walk walk
1 + 2 + 3   1 2 3

The Eighth Note Rest Song

Count out loud as you play this piece.
This will help you play the rhythms correctly.

Lento (Slow)

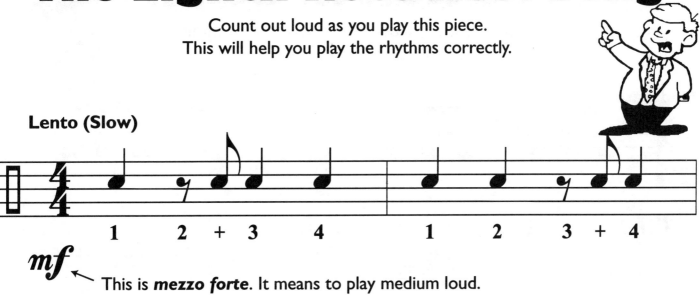

mf ← This is **mezzo forte**. It means to play medium loud.

f The volume changes to **forte** here. Play a little louder than **mezzo forte**.

The Review Song!

Here is a song that has many of the things
we learned so far. Have fun!

Moderato

mf

f

Let's Play the Drum Set!

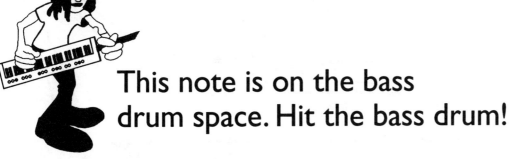

This note is on the bass drum space. Hit the bass drum!

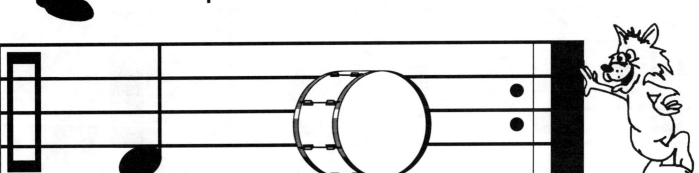

This note is on the snare drum space. Hit the snare drum!

This note is on the hi hat line. Hit the hi hat!

24

Now, hit the snare drum and hi hat together.

Now, hit the hi hat, snare and bass drum together!

It's Rock and Roll Time!

1. Play these notes. Remember, this is the bass drum and hi hat together.

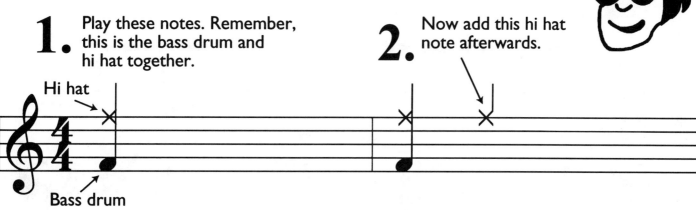

2. Now add this hi hat note afterwards.

3. Now these three...

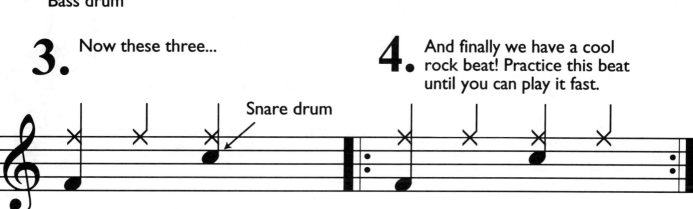

4. And finally we have a cool rock beat! Practice this beat until you can play it fast.

Here is another fun beat!

Try playing these quarter notes slowly.

5.
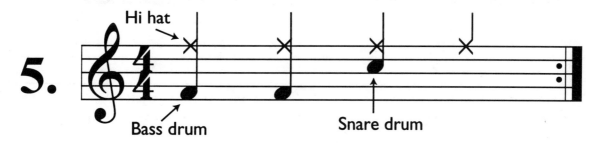

Now try playing this eighth note pattern. It's the same pattern as number 5, only faster!

6.
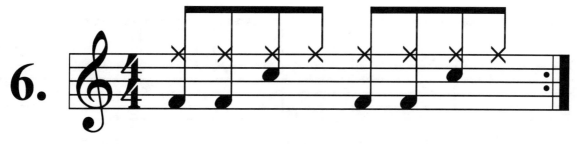

Let's Learn More Rock Beats!

Practice each beat very slowly and carefully. Once you can play all the way through a measure perfectly, then you can try playing it a little faster.

Hi, I'm Miss Drumberger.
Rockin' Rob is out with the flu.

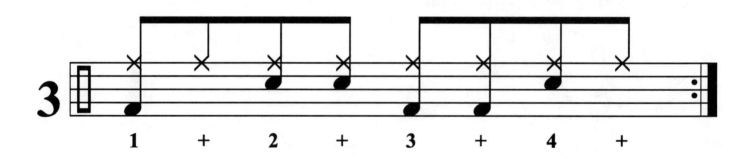

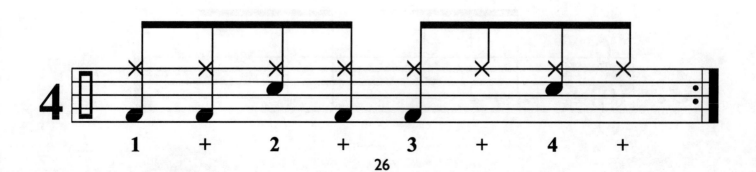

26

Let's Learn Even More Rock Beats!

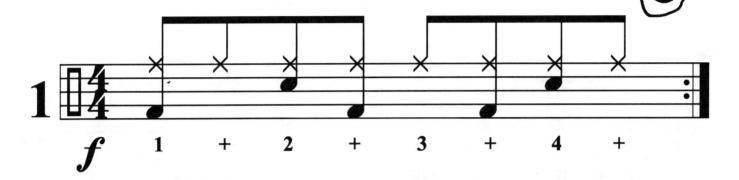

f 1 + 2 + 3 + 4 +

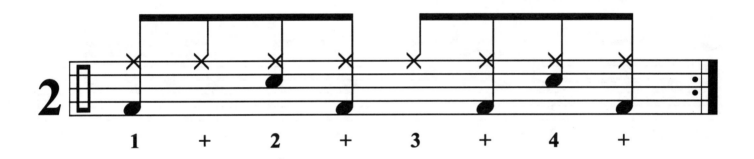

1 + 2 + 3 + 4 +

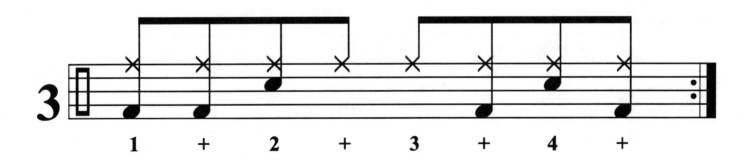

1 + 2 + 3 + 4 +

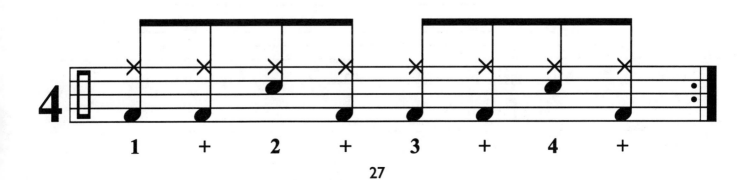

1 + 2 + 3 + 4 +

Sixteenth Notes

These are sixteenth notes. They are twice as fast as eighth notes.
Count them out loud saying "Miss-iss-ipp-i" or "one-e-and-a"

1.

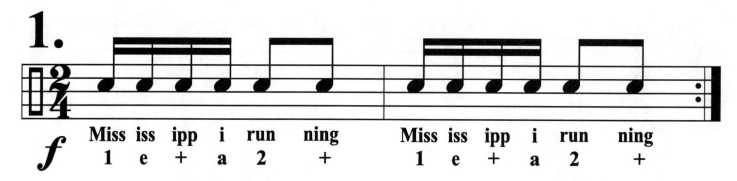

Miss	iss	ipp	i	run	ning		Miss	iss	ipp	i	run	ning
1	e	+	a	2	+		1	e	+	a	2	+

f

Count out loud!

2.

run	ning	Miss	iss	ipp	i		run	ning	Miss	iss	ipp	i
1	+	2	e	+	a		1	+	2	e	+	a

3.

Miss	iss	ipp	i	walk		Miss	iss	ipp	i	walk
1	e	+	a	2		1	e	+	a	2

4.

walk	Miss	iss	ipp	i		walk	Miss	iss	ipp	i
1	2	e	+	a		1	2	e	+	a

More Sixteenth Notes

The exercises on this page are each two measures long.
Practice each one until you can play it easily.

1.

Miss	iss	ipp	i	Miss	iss	ipp	i	run	ning	Miss	iss	ipp	i
1	e	+	a	2	e	+	a	1	+	2	e	+	a

f

Count out loud!

2.

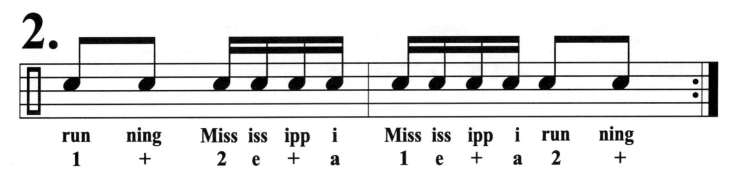

run	ning	Miss	iss	ipp	i	Miss	iss	ipp	i	run	ning
1	+	2	e	+	a	1	e	+	a	2	+

3.

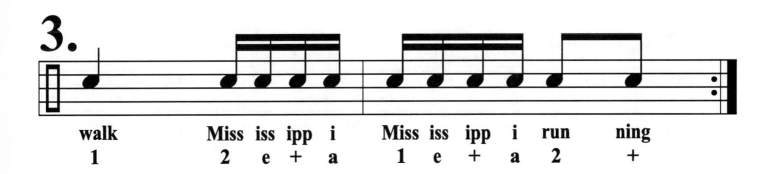

walk	Miss	iss	ipp	i	Miss	iss	ipp	i	run	ning
1	2	e	+	a	1	e	+	a	2	+

4.

run	ning	Miss	iss	ipp	i	Miss	iss	ipp	i	walk
1	+	2	e	+	a	1	e	+	a	2

Sixteenth Note March

When you play this page, count out loud. Halfway through the piece, the
dynamics (volume) change from piano (soft) to forte (loud).

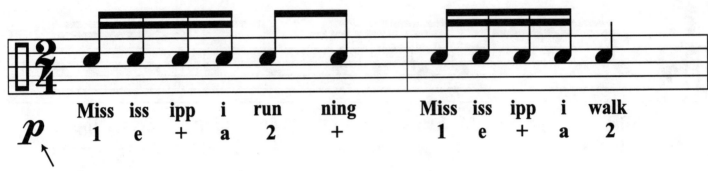

This means *piano* — play softly.

Now play *forte* — loud!

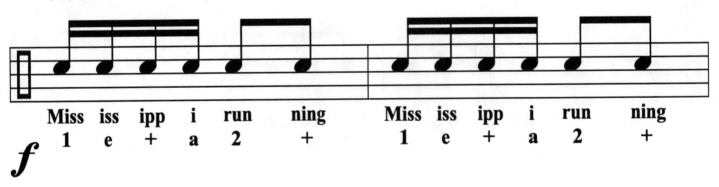

Sixteenth Notes in Three Four

Count out loud and use the sticking written underneath the notes.

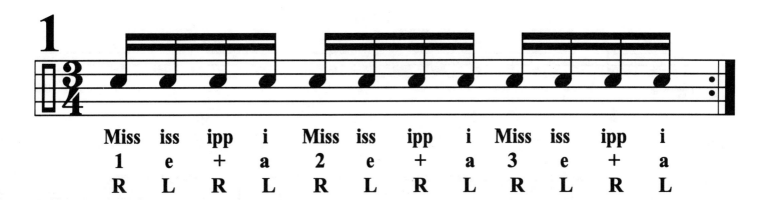

Miss	iss	ipp	i	Miss	iss	ipp	i	Miss	iss	ipp	i
1	e	+	a	2	e	+	a	3	e	+	a
R	L	R	L	R	L	R	L	R	L	R	L

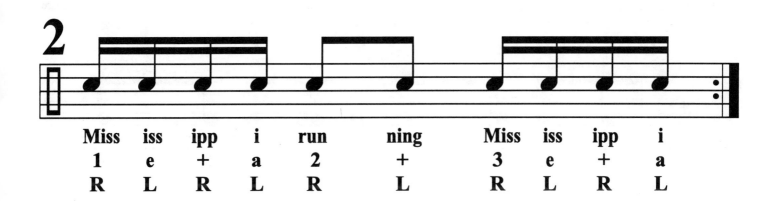

Miss	iss	ipp	i	run	ning	Miss	iss	ipp	i
1	e	+	a	2	+	3	e	+	a
R	L	R	L	R	L	R	L	R	L

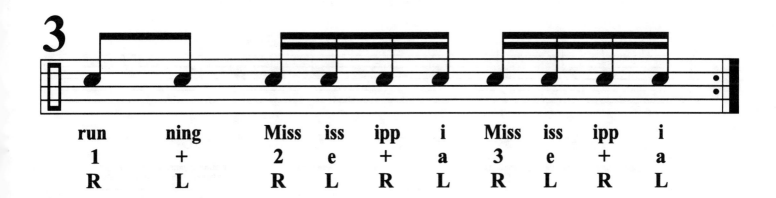

run	ning	Miss	iss	ipp	i	Miss	iss	ipp	i
1	+	2	e	+	a	3	e	+	a
R	L	R	L	R	L	R	L	R	L

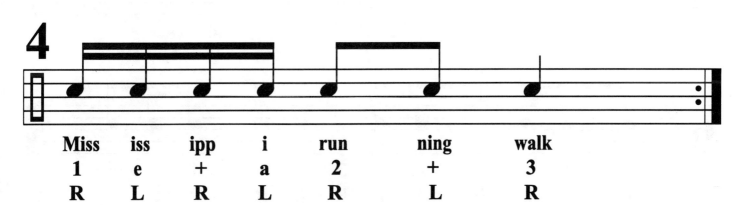

Miss	iss	ipp	i	run	ning	walk
1	e	+	a	2	+	3
R	L	R	L	R	L	R

We Can Combine Eighth and Sixteenth Notes

Count out loud.

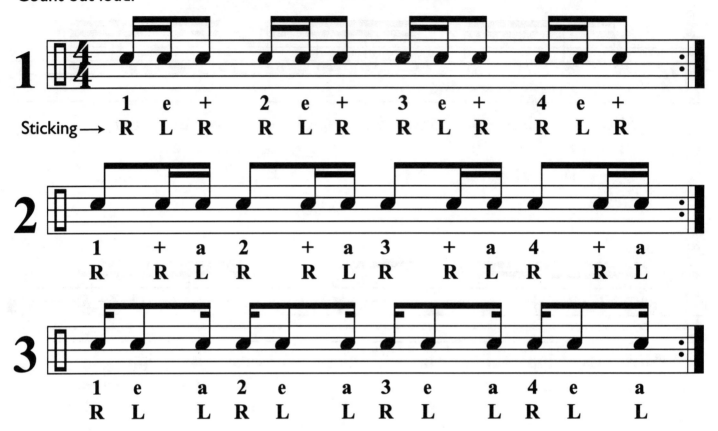

1

1	e	+	2	e	+	3	e	+	4	e	+

Sticking → R L R R L R R L R R L R

2

1		+	a	2		+	a	3		+	a	4		+	a

R R L R R L R R L R R L

3

1	e		a	2	e		a	3	e		a	4	e		a

R L L L R L L R L L L R L L L L

The next three exercises combine some of the things you have learned.

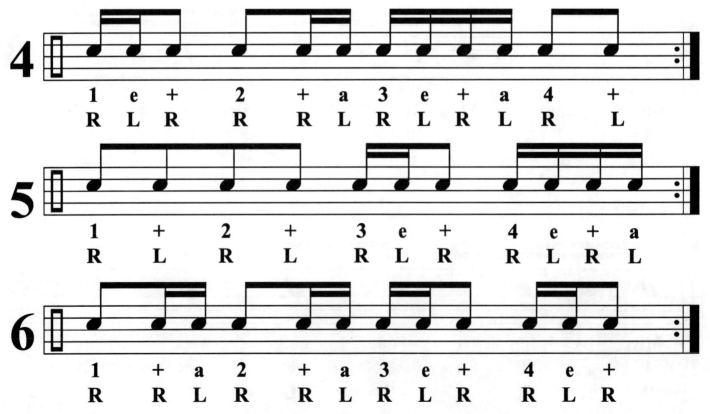

4

1 e + 2 + a 3 e + a 4 +
R L R R R L R L R L R L

5

1 + 2 + 3 e + 4 e + a
R L R L R L R R L R L

6

1 + a 2 + a 3 e + 4 e +
R R L R R L R L R L R R L R

32

Introducing the Sixteenth Rest

This is a sixteenth rest. A sixteenth rest is a silent sixteenth note.

This is a single sixteenth note. It has two flags on it representing the two beams of the sixteenth notes.

1

1 e + 2 e + 3 e + 4 e +

Sticking → R L R R L R R L R R L R

2

1 E + a 2 E + a 3 E + a 4 E + a

R R L R R L R R L R R L

3

1 e + a 2 e + a 3 e + a 4 e + a

R L L R L L R L L R L L

4

1 e + a 2 e + a 3 e + a 4 e + a

L R L L R L L R L L R L

5

1 e + a 2 e + a 3 e + a 4 e + a

R L R L R L R L

The Sixteenth Note Review

This song has many of the rhythms we have learned so far. If you have trouble playing it, go back a few pages and practice all of the sixteenth note exercises again.

35

Sixteenths on the Set

Play exercise number one fifty times before you try number two.
Remember, sixteenth notes are played twice as fast as eighth notes.

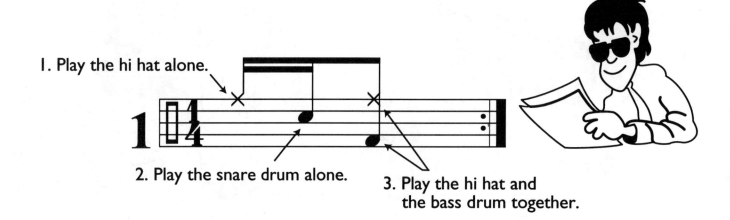

1. Play the hi hat alone.

2. Play the snare drum alone.

3. Play the hi hat and
   the bass drum together.

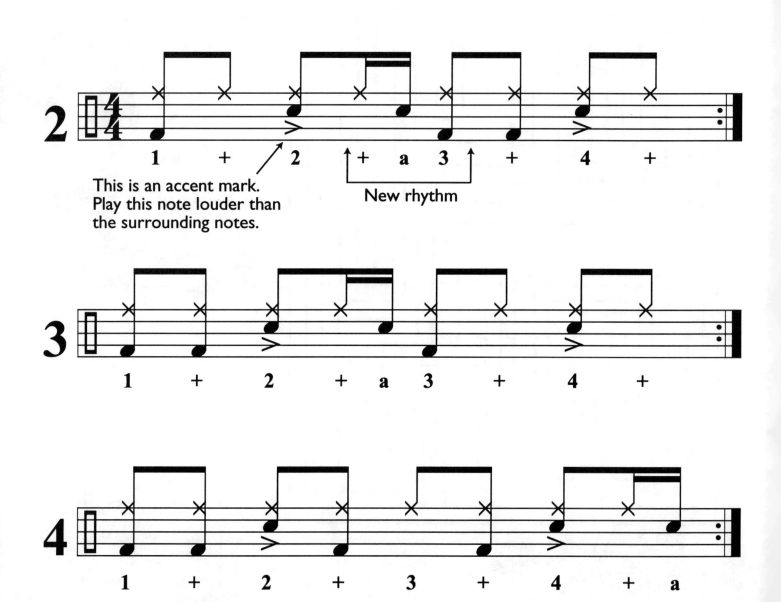

This is an accent mark.
Play this note louder than
the surrounding notes.

New rhythm

Sixteenth Notes on the Bass Drum

Practice this exercise over and over until you can play it fast. Try positioning your foot halfway down the foot pedal and lift your heel up. This way you can use your whole leg to hit the bass drum loudly.

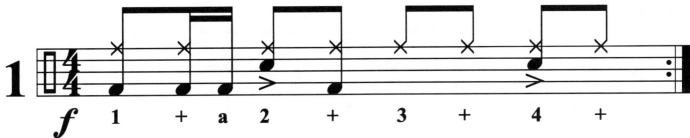

1. Bass and hi hat together

2. Bass drum alone

3. Snare and bass together.

Here are some fun beats using your new bass drum skill!

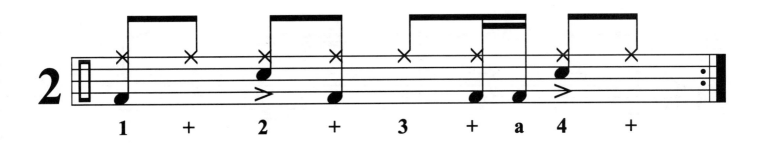

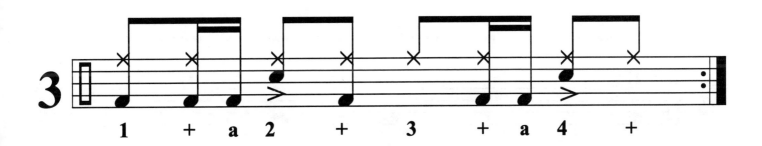

A New Rhythm for the Bass Drum

Practice exercise number one until you can play it easily. Then try the others.

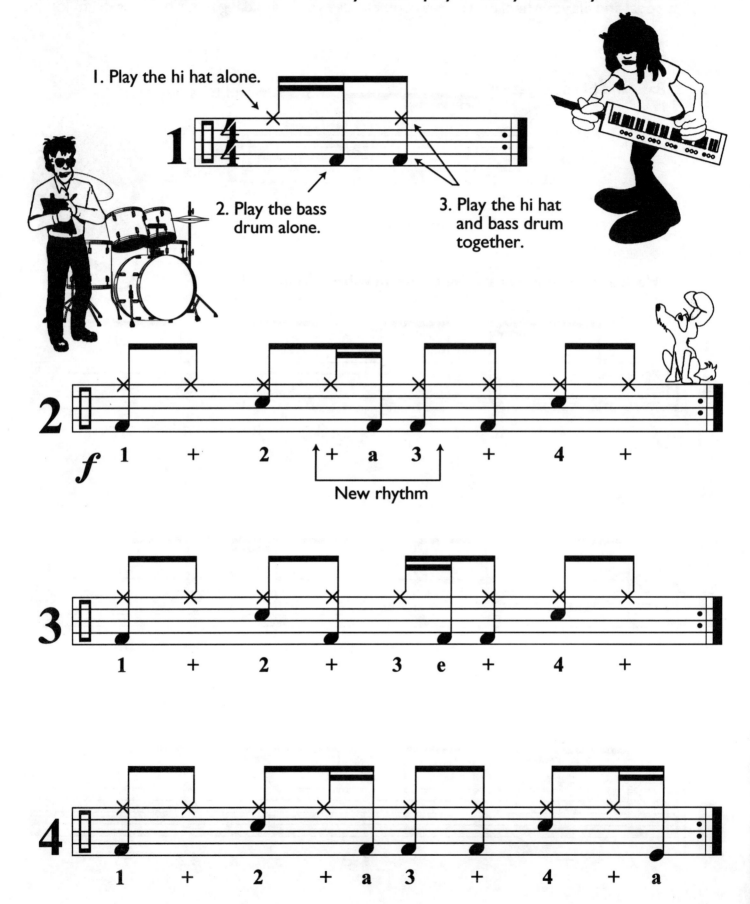

Another Cool Drum Pattern!

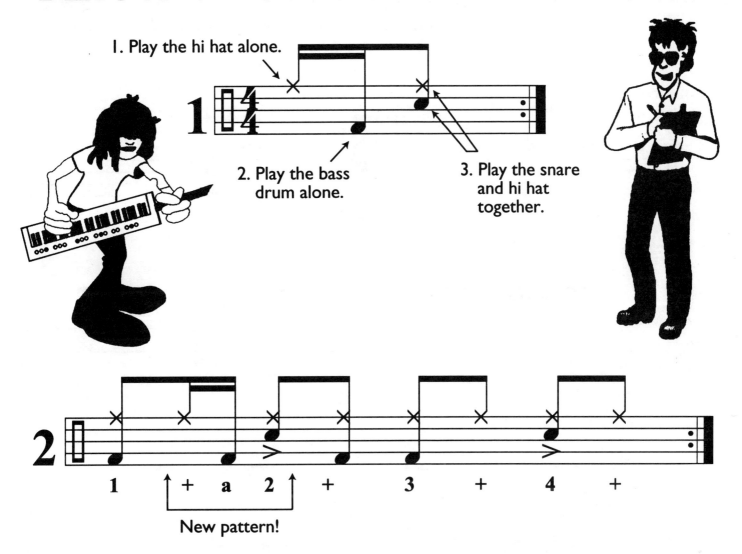

1. Play the hi hat alone.

2. Play the bass drum alone.

3. Play the snare and hi hat together.

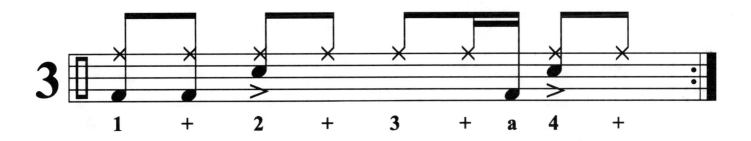

1   +   a   2   +   3   +   4   +

New pattern!

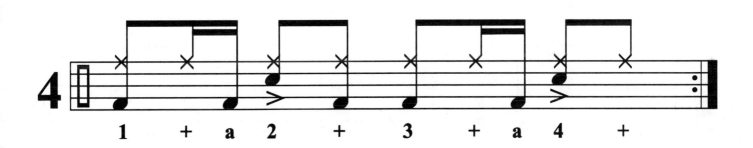

1   +   2   +   3   +   a   4   +

1   +   a   2   +   3   +   a   4   +

Bonus Beats

The bonus beats are combinations of the things you have learned so far.
Pay careful attention to the accents on the snare drum.

Allegro
(brisk, lively)

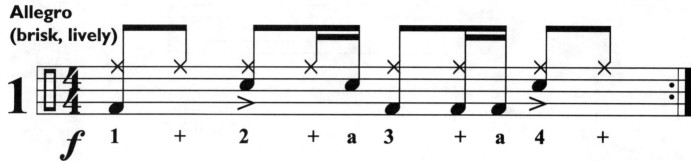

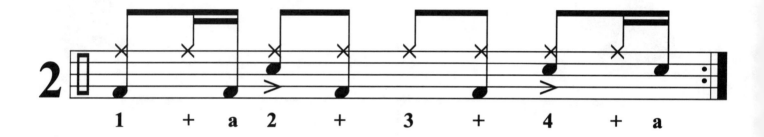

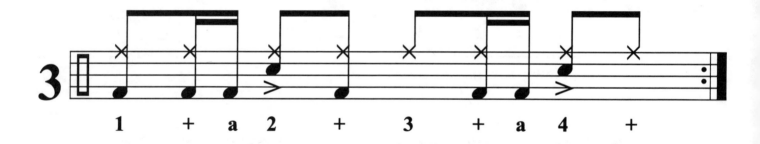

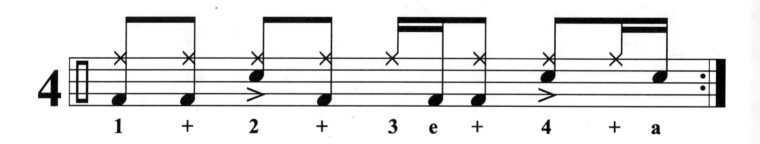

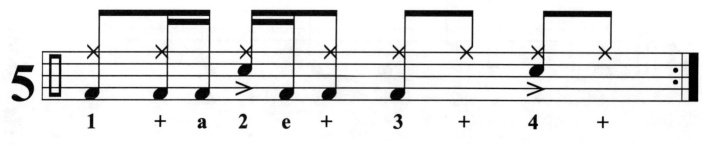

More Bonus Beats

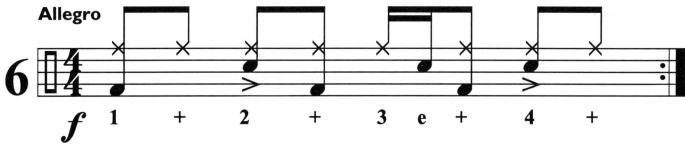

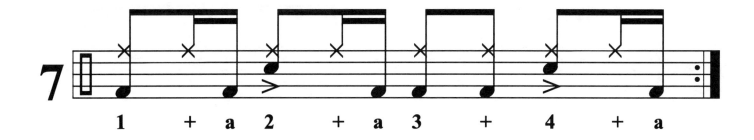

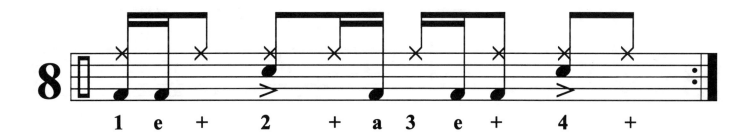

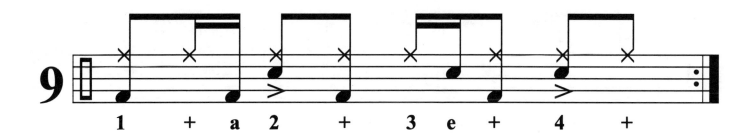

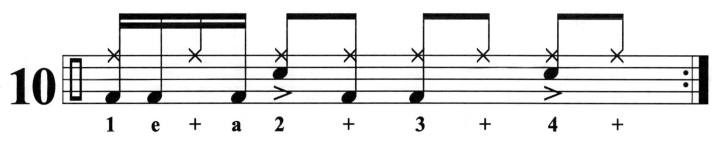

Even More Bonus Beats!

Allegro

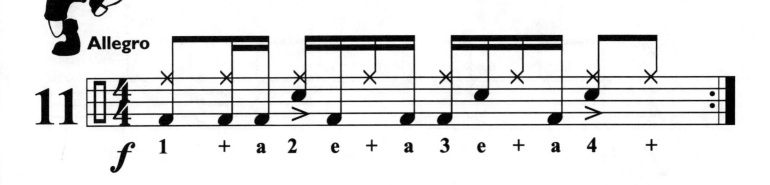

11 f 1 + a 2 e + a 3 e + a 4 +

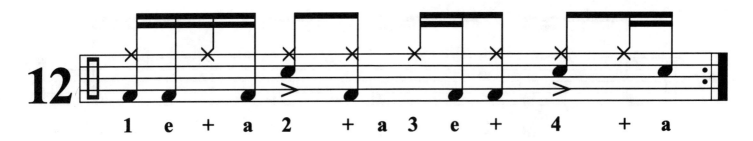

12 1 e + a 2 + a 3 e + 4 + a

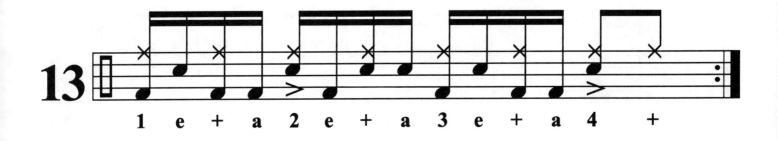

13 1 e + a 2 e + a 3 e + a 4 +

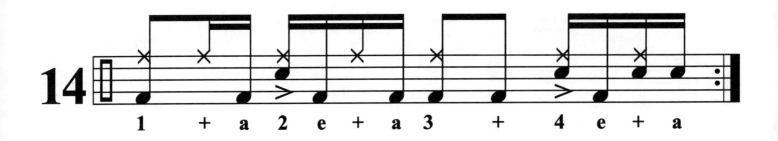

14 1 + a 2 e + a 3 + 4 e + a

15 1 e + a 2 e + a 3 e + a 4 +

Sixteenth Notes on the Hi Hat

This type of beat is called the halftime groove. Play each exercise slowly at first. Try to keep your hi hat hand relaxed and loose as you play these exercises. If you tense up you will restrict the blood flow to your forearm muscles and tire quickly.

Right hand

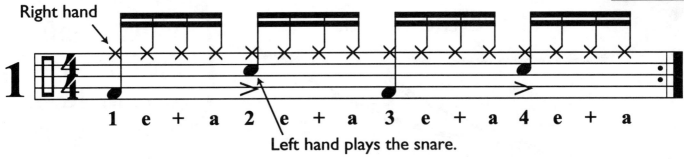

1 e + a 2 e + a 3 e + a 4 e + a

Left hand plays the snare.

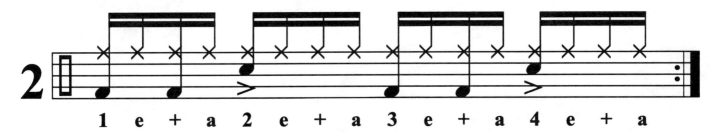

1 e + a 2 e + a 3 e + a 4 e + a

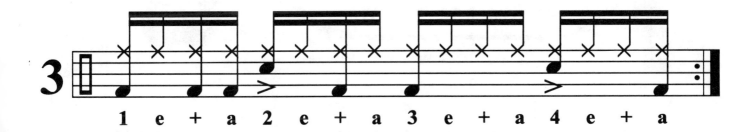

1 e + a 2 e + a 3 e + a 4 e + a

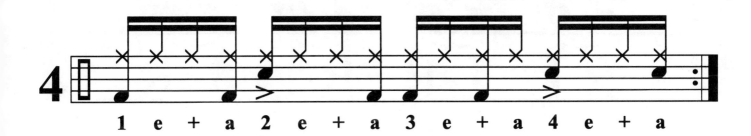

1 e + a 2 e + a 3 e + a 4 e + a

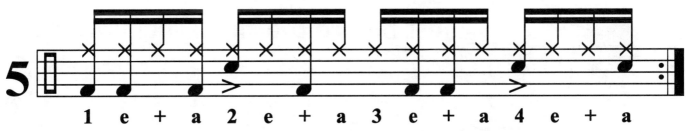

1 e + a 2 e + a 3 e + a 4 e + a

43

Let's Learn the Flam!

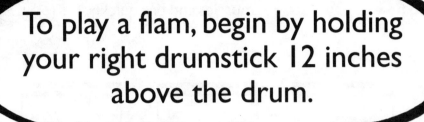

To play a flam, begin by holding your right drumstick 12 inches above the drum.

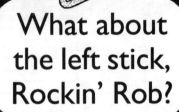

What about the left stick, Rockin' Rob?

Hold the left stick about three inches above the drum.

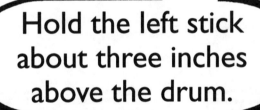

R L L R R L L R

Drop both sticks at the same time allowing the left stick to hit just before the right. Then switch.

44

The Flam Song

Practice playing this page slowly at first.
Concentrate on playing the flams perfectly.
Then try it a little faster!

Tempo di marcia

Sticking R R L L r L L R R L R L L R
p 1 2 + 3 4 1 2 + 3 + 4

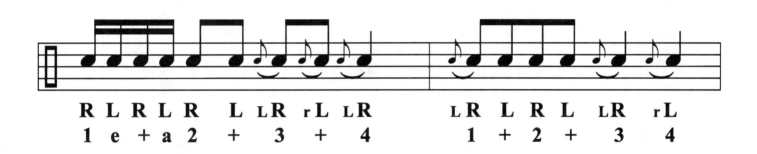

R L R L R L L R r L L R L R L R L L R r L
1 e + a 2 + 3 + 4 1 + 2 + 3 4

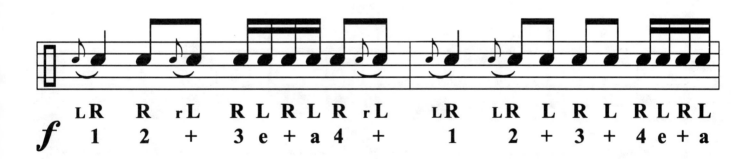

L R R r L R L R L R r L L R L R L R L R L R L
f 1 2 + 3 e + a 4 + 1 2 + 3 + 4 e + a

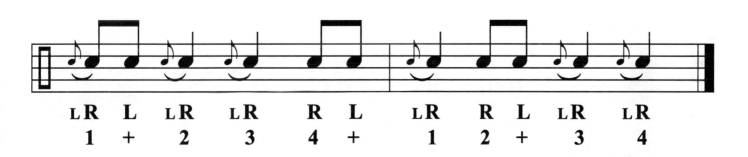

L R L L R L R R L L R R L L R L R
1 + 2 3 4 + 1 2 + 3 4

45

Let's Learn the Drag!

The proper way to play a drag is similar to a flam. Hold your right stick three inches above the drum.

And hold your left stick 6 inches above the drum.

The lower stick strikes twice just before the upper stick.

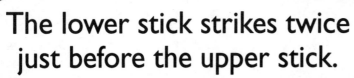

R R L L L L R R R L L L R

Practice by playing twenty drags a day.

Boy, that sounds like a drag!

The Drag Song

Concentrate on playing the drags perfectly.
The bounced notes should be played softly.
Watch for the dynamics (volume marks).

Tempo di marcia

R   LLR   L   R   LLR   L   R   rrL   LLR   L   R   L

ff ← This is *fortissimo*.
It means to play at
a very loud volume!

R   L   rrL   LLR   L   R   R L R L R   L   rrL

mf

LLR   LLR   L   R L R L R   L   LLR   L   R   L   LLR   L   R L R L

p < **ff**

R   L   LLR   L   R L R L R   L   R   LLR   rr L

ff _____ *p* **ff** **fff** fortissimo
extremely loud!

47

The Flam and Drag March

Watch for the dynamic changes, and repeat marks!

Tempo di marcia

f

ff

p

This is a *ritornello* sign. When you see this, repeat the previous measure.

mf

ff — *fff*

48

49

Fun With Fills

We are going to practice drumset fills. Fills make our drum parts sound more exciting! Many songs are made of four measure phrases and that's how we will practice our fills.

This fill is in four four time. You can play fills in every time signature, but the fill must fit the number of beats allowed in a measure.

Practice playing this fill using single strokes (R, L, R, L), and try to play it strongly and evenly.

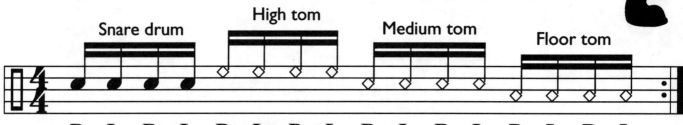

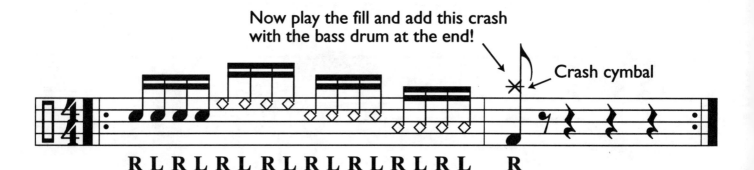

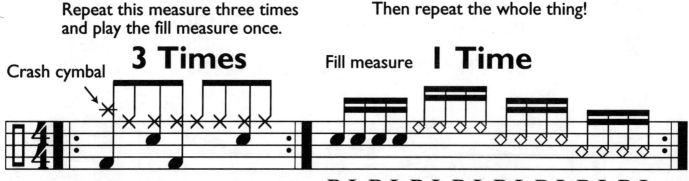

50

Try These Cool Fills

After you have practiced each fill and can play it fast, try it in a four measure phrase. Play three measures of a pattern from page 26 and one measure of a fill from this page. After each fill, crash on beat one and play the whole thing again!

1

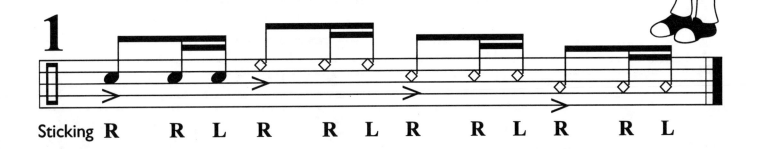

Sticking **R   R L R   R L R   R L R   R L**

2

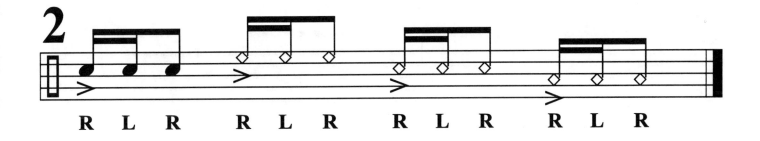

R L R   R L R   R L R   R L R

3

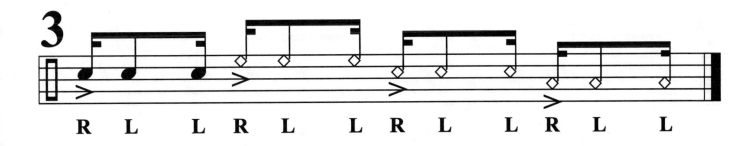

R L   L R L   L R L   L R L   L

4

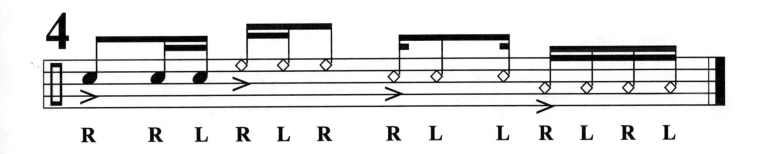

R   R L R L R   R L L   L R L R L

51

Let's Learn Six Eight Time

6 Remember, the top number of the time signature tells you how many beats are in a measure. In this case, six!

8 The bottom number tells you what kind of note we are calling a beat. There are six eighth notes in each measure.

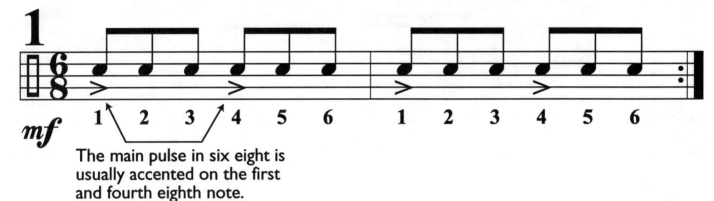

The main pulse in six eight is usually accented on the first and fourth eighth note.

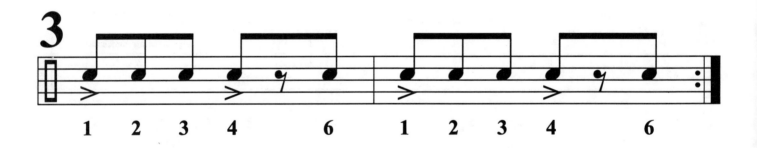

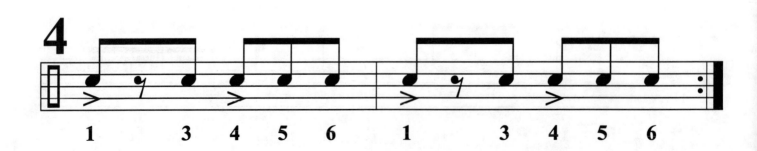

Six Eight March

Tempo di marcia

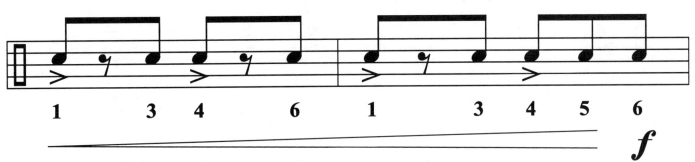

This is a *crescendo* mark. It means to get gradually louder.

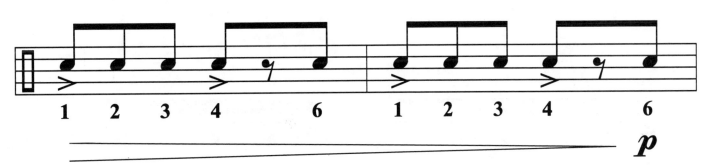

This is a *decrescendo* mark. It means to get gradually softer.

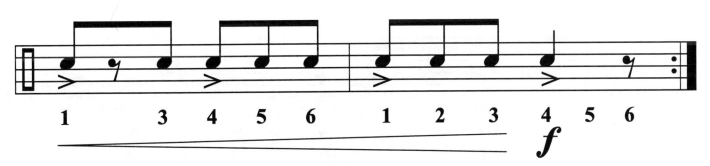

I Like Sixteenth Notes in Six Eight

Sixteenth notes are twice as fast as eighth notes. In each measure there are 6 eighth notes. That means we can have 12 sixteenth notes because 12 is twice as much as 6!

Andante (medium slow)

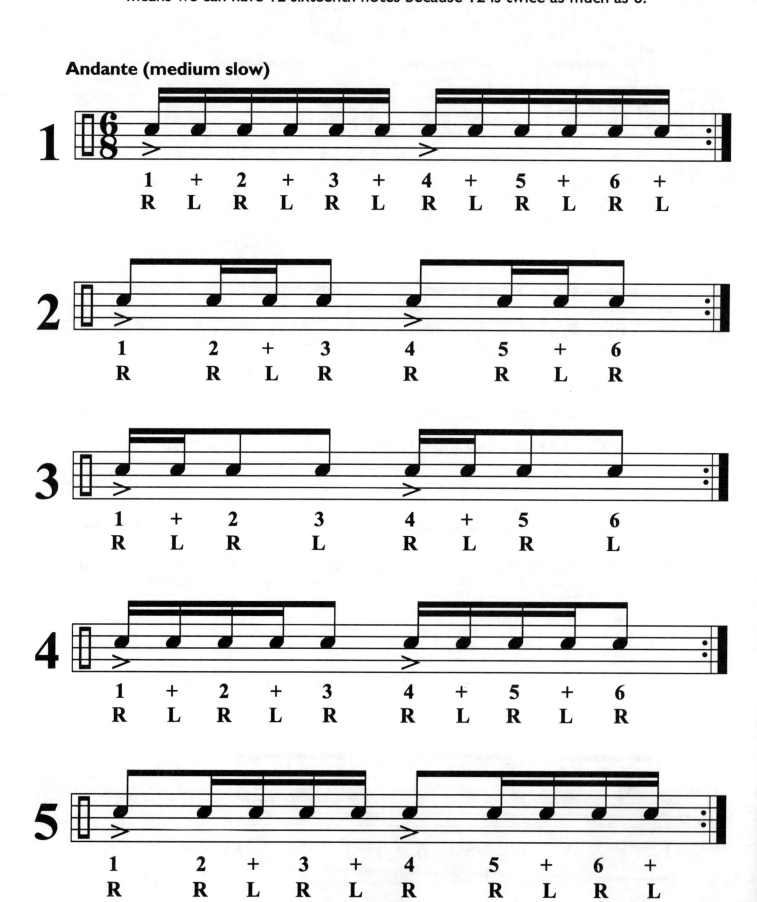

The Six Eight Sixteenth Song

Watch for the dynamics!

Andante

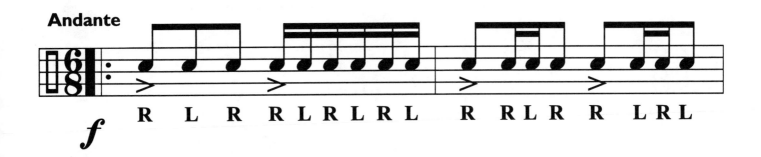

pp ← This is *pianissimo*.
Play very softly.

Six Eight Drumset Beats are Fun!

In six eight time, there are six eighth notes in each measure.
This kind of beat sounds great when playing rock and blues music!

Six Eight Fills

Practice each fill until you can play it easily. Then play three measures of a six-eight beat and one measure of fill. This will make a four measure phrase. Hit the crash cymbal on beat one after the fill.

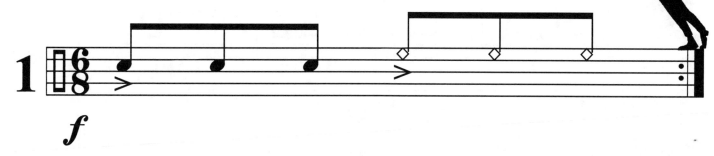

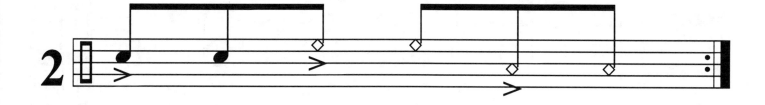

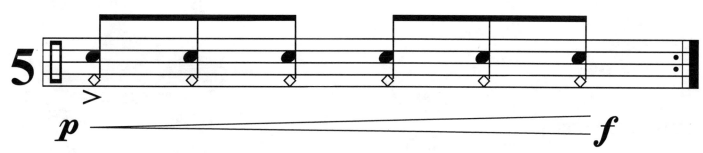

Mike's Musical Mix Up

E	A	D	G	E	C	I	T	C	A	R	P	I	D
T	O	E	C	N	D	T	N	E	S	A	N	D	E
O	N	I	I	E	G	R	A	W	L	C	R	Q	A
N	M	L	R	I	O	I	U	L	U	A	A	O	A
F	E	S	E	S	G	I	E	M	U	R	M	O	T
I	M	O	S	D	T	N	R	G	S	O	O	B	S
L	I	L	U	D	R	U	M	S	I	T	O	Y	E
L	L	A	B	M	Y	C	Y	M	B	A	L	H	R
M	G	T	H	B	E	A	T	F	N	L	B	C	A
E	N	A	G	E	L	E	E	E	E	I	A	T	S
E	I	R	I	H	I	H	A	T	L	N	S	C	N
N	O	Y	B	U	R	E	D	O	M	O	S	H	I
E	D	E	N	I	F	N	O	C	N	U	O	E	C
P	A	R	F	L	E	L	O	M	H	T	Y	H	R

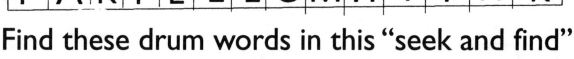

Find these drum words in this "seek and find"

Fill   Drums
Practice   Rest
Note   Hi hat
Rhythm   Cymbal
Beat   Snare
Drumstick   Bass
Tom

Anybody hungry?

58

What are Triplets?

Triplets are notes that are played in groups of three!
The top notes are regular eighth notes…

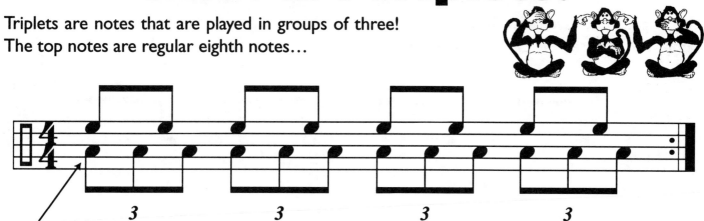

The bottom notes are *triplets*. See how there are three triplet notes for every two regular eighth notes? Now try the examples below.

1

Count 1 + 2 + 3 trip let 4 trip let

2

1 + 2 trip let 3 + 4 trip let

3

1 trip let 2 + 3 trip let 4 +

4

1 trip let 2 trip let 3 + 4 +

Can Triplets Have Rests?

Yes! Triplets can have rests. Rests are silent notes and can be grouped as triplets the same way as notes. We can combine them to make some very fun rhythms!

1   let   2   let   3   let   4   let

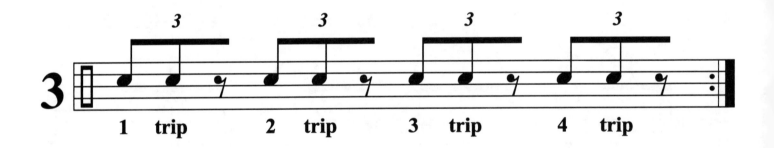

trip let   trip let   trip let   trip let

1 trip   2 trip   3 trip   4 trip

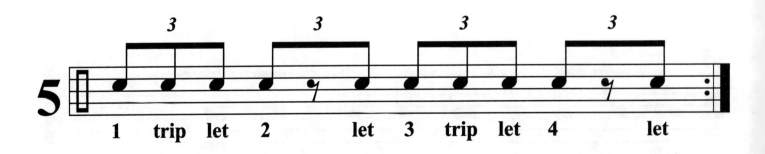

1   let 2 trip let 3   let 4 trip let

1 trip let 2   let 3 trip let 4   let

The Shuffle Beat

This beat is played with eighth notes and eighth note rests. Notice that the Hi hat is played on the "1" and the "Let." An eighth note rest is in the middle of each beat.

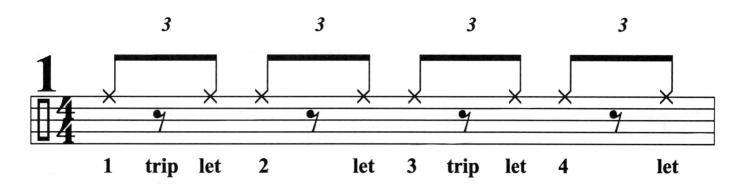

1   trip   let   2   let   3   trip   let   4   let

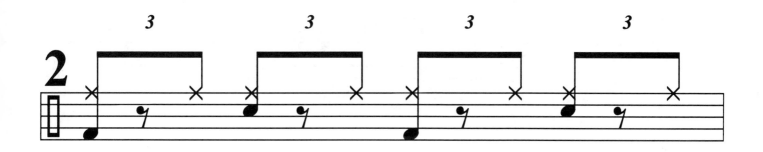

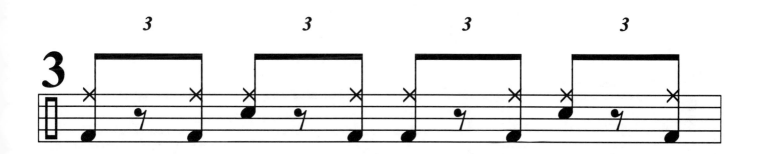

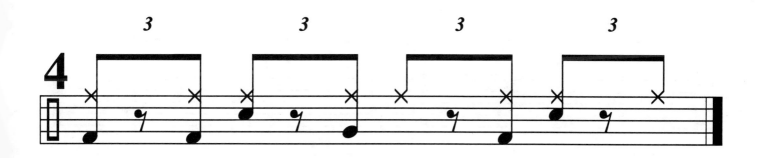

Halftime Shuffle Dance Grooves

This Hi hat rhythm is the same as the Shuffle Beat.
The snare drum is played on beat 3 instead of 2 and 4.
Make sure that you keep the triplet feel going the whole time you practice these patterns!

Triplet Fills Are Groups of Three

Practice each fill and when you're ready, play it in a four measure phrase.
These fills sound great with the shuffle beats.

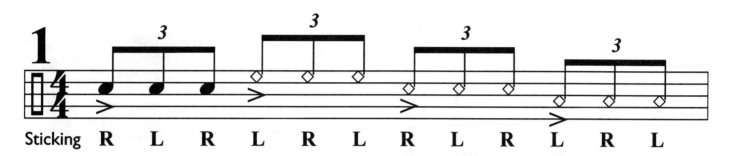

Sticking R L R L R L R L R L R L

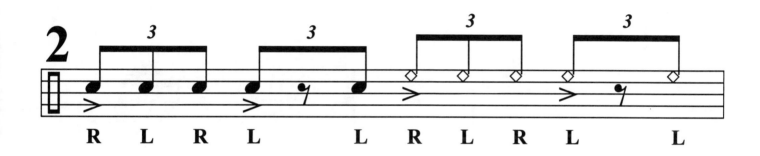

R L R L L R L R L L

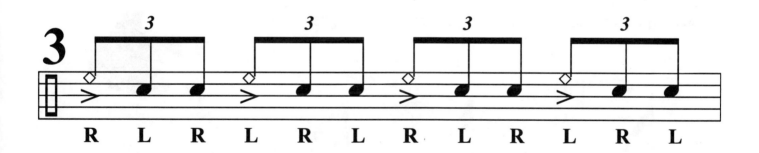

R L R L R L R L R L R L

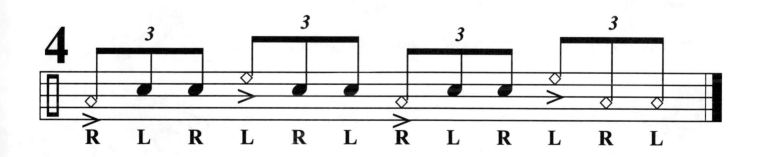

R L R L R L R L R L R L R L

Dotted Notes Are Great!

A dot set after a note adds half the value of the note to the note.

This is a dotted half note. Half its value is a quarter note.

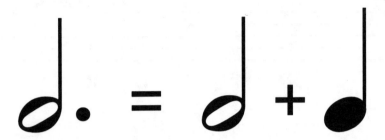

A dotted half note is equal to a half note plus a quarter note.

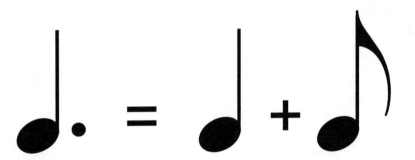

A dotted quarter note is equal to a quarter plus an eighth note.

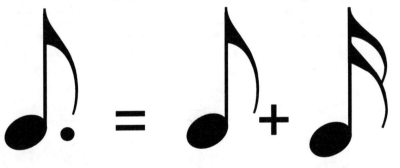

A dotted eighth note is equal to an eighth plus a sixteenth.

Let's Play Dotted Rhythms

This page demonstrates how dotted notes fit into four four
and six eight. Play each exercise and count out loud.
Look at the time signature of each one before you play it.

1
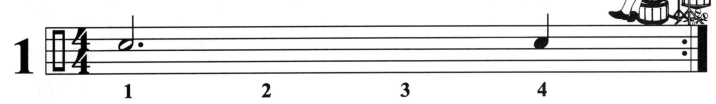

2
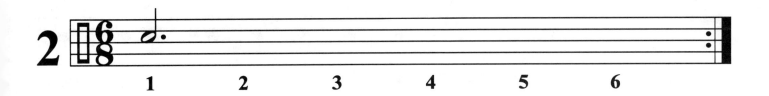

3

4
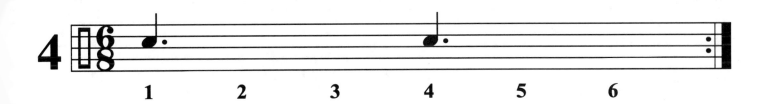

5

6

The Dotted Note March

Notice the repeat barline at the beginning and end of this song. This means to play the whole piece twice. To learn this song, try studying each measure separately first and then play the whole page.

fff This is *fortissimo*. Play extremely loud!

66

Dotted Notes In Six Eight

A dotted quarter note is equal to 3 eighth notes so it can count as half of a measure.

Dotted rests work the same way as notes!

These repeat barlines tell you to play these two measures twice.

Let's Learn the 5 Stroke Roll!

RRLLR LLRRL

Practice playing the five stroke roll. When you get it fast, the sticks should bounce.

Warm up with your double stroke roll and it will help your five stroke rolls.

OUCH!

Reading Five Stroke Rolls

This is a five stroke roll written as thirty-second notes.
Remember to bounce the first four notes like a double stroke roll.

Five stroke rolls written like this are very common.
When you see this, play it like the example above.

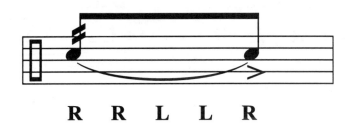

Practice playing this exercise to get used to playing five stroke rolls.

The Five Stroke Roll March

Watch for the dynamic marks and accents.

Tempo di marcia

R L R L R RRLLR R L R L R L RRLLR R

RRLLR R L R L R L R L RRLLR R L R L R L R

R R R L R L RRLLR R R L R L

Here is a **repeat** mark. Go back to the beginning and play it again.

R L R L R RRLLR R L R L R RRLLR RRLLR R

70

Two Hands on the Hi Hat

To play these patterns, play the hi hat with both hands.

The sticking pattern is a single stroke roll. The right hand goes back and fourth between the hi hat and the snare!

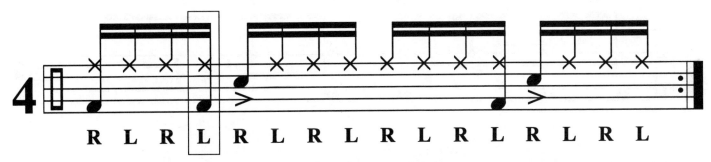

Notice that the left hand strikes the hi hat as you play the bass drum.

Let's Open and Close the Hi Hat

Use your left foot to open the hi hat whenever you see an "O" over a hi hat note. You must hit it while it is open so it rings!

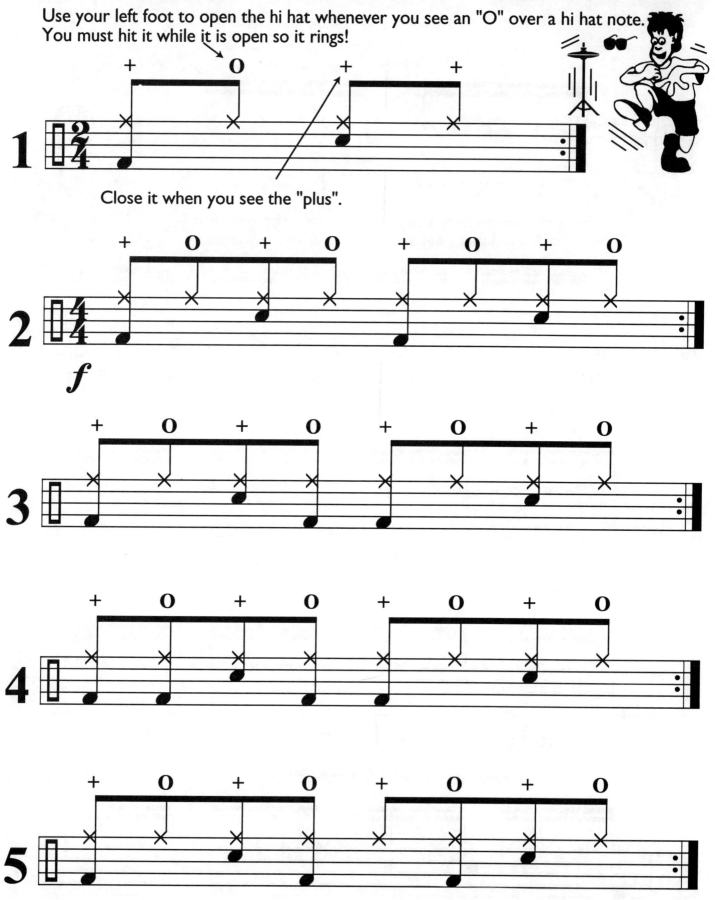

Close it when you see the "plus".

72

Etudes for Eighth Rests

Notice the sixth line. Here we have a first and second ending. The first time through, play the first ending measure and go back to the repeat mark at the beginning of the line. Play the passage again, this time skip the first ending and play the second ending measure.

73

I'm a Drumming Fool

In four-four time, a half rest gets 2 counts. Do not confuse it with a whole rest.
A half rest sits on top of the line. A whole rest hangs below the line.

I Lost My Drum When You Sneezed

Write in the beats underneath the notes before you play this piece.
This will help you analyze the rhythms.

The Challenge *sfz* = Strongly accented

75

Three-Four, Knock on the Door!

Bis means "twice". The measures within the bracket should be played twice.

Andante

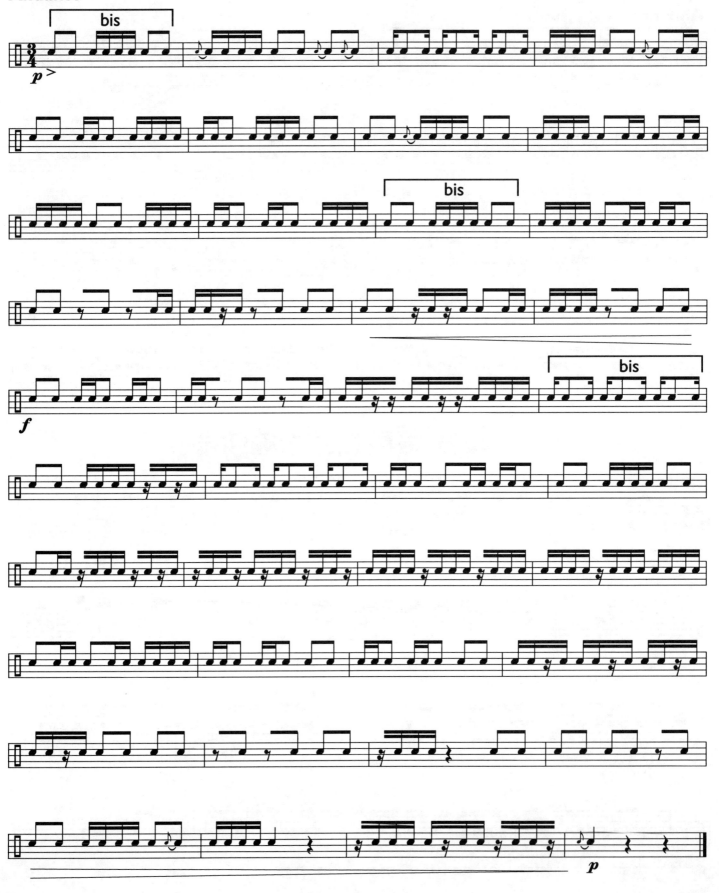

The Twelve-Eight Song

Each twelve-eight measure can be counted as 4 beats.
The dotted eighth note receives one beat.

The Challenge

The Super Flam Jam

The natural tendency is to accent flammed notes. These notes should not be accented unless an accent mark is indicated. The purpose of a flam is to thicken a note, not to make it louder.

Andante

Drag Those Sticks Around!

The natural tendency is to accent drags. Drags should not be accented unless an accent mark is indicated. The purpose of a drag is to broaden the note, not to make it louder.

Andante

Five Stroke Roll Solo

The natural tendency is to accent the last note of a 5 stroke roll. Do not accent the note unless an accent mark is indicated. Try to play the single last note the same volume as the rest of the roll.

Moderato

The Playalong Section

Hi, there. Musical Mike here to tell you about the playalong songs.
Every song has a different beat. Listen to each song before you try to play it. Then listen to it again and follow along with the written drum part. It helps to point to each measure as you go. When you are ready, try playing to the version with the drums and then to the version without the drums. Caution: use ear protection. When you turn up the music loud and play the drums to it, the sound can cause ear damage! Foam ear plugs or protective headphones are good.

The Notation Key

You will need to refer to this chart while learning the playalong songs because there are a few new notes.

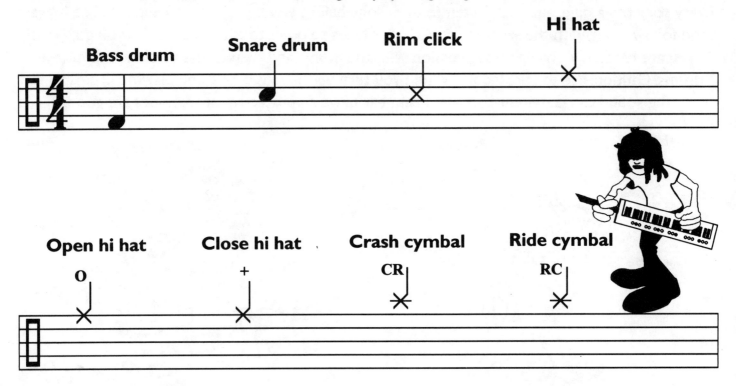

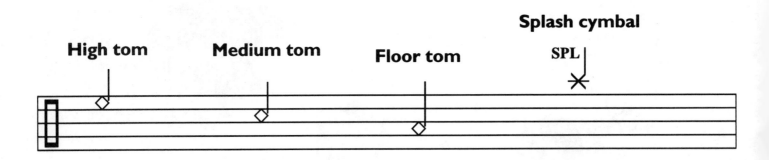

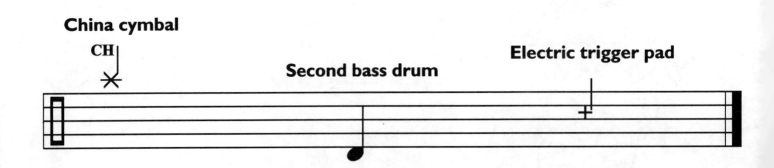

Clearwater

Mike Silverman

Bass Solo

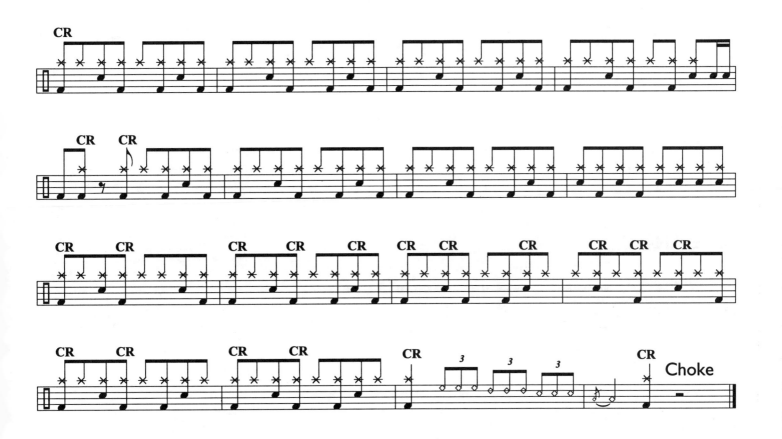

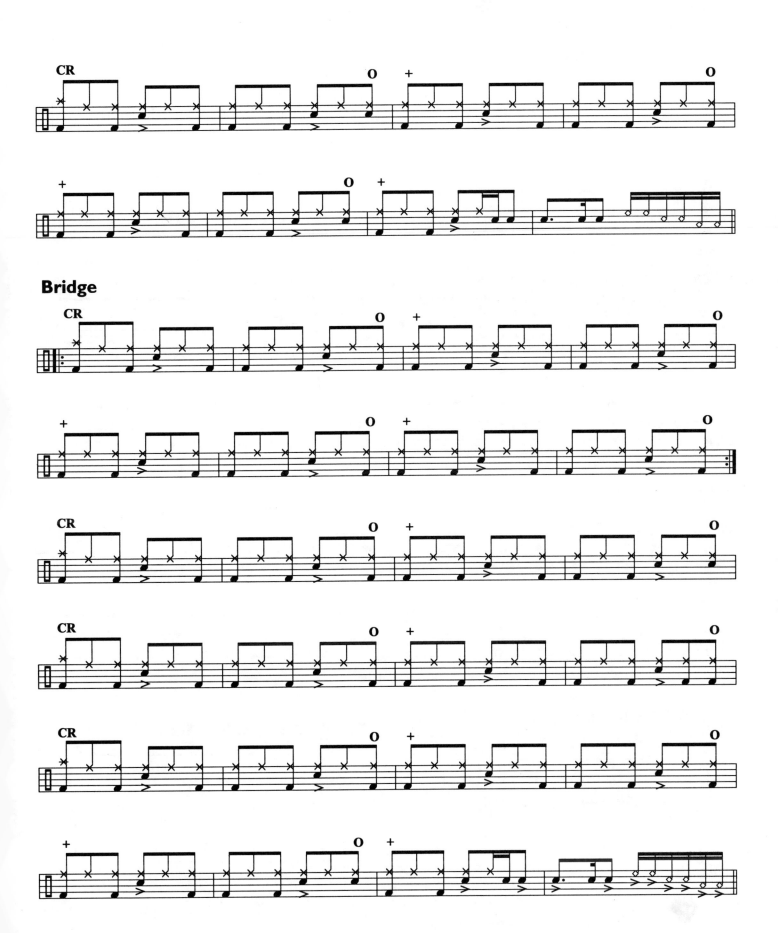

Bridge

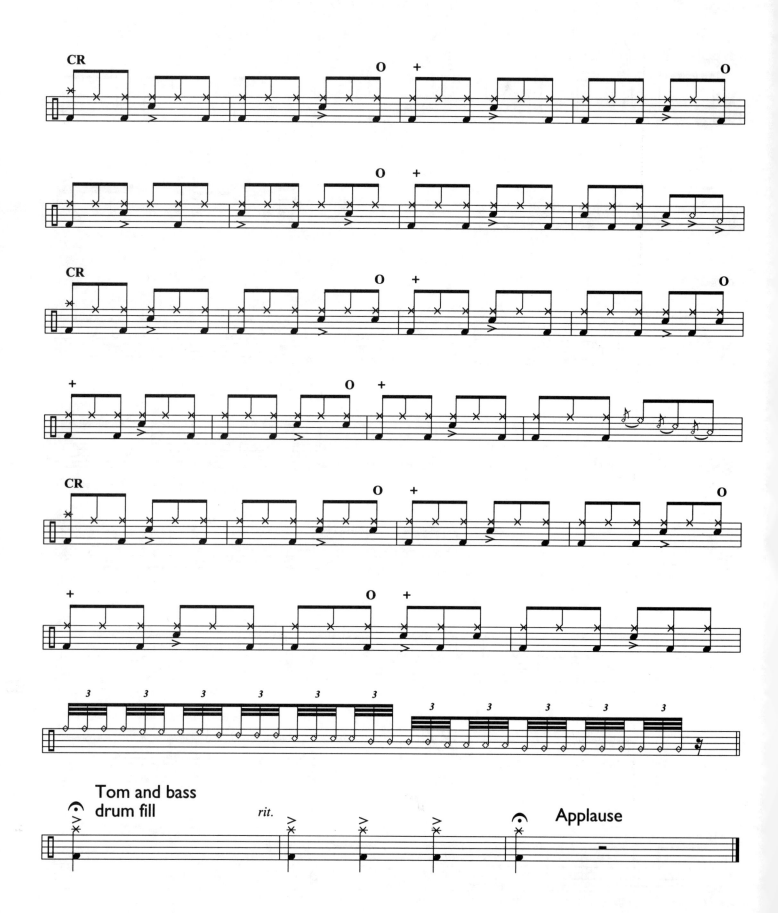

Tennessee

Banjo Introduction
Drums Tacet, don't play

Mike Silverman

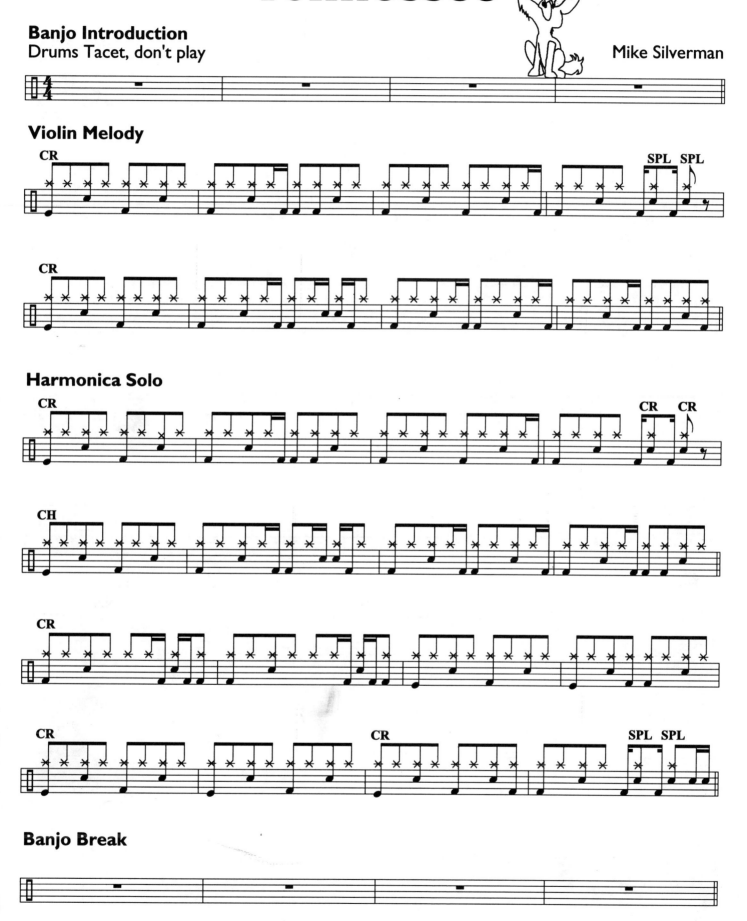

Violin Melody

Harmonica Solo

Banjo Break

Violin

Mikey G

Musical Mike's Theme

Intro

Mike Silverman

Theme Melody

Tenor Sax Solo

Piano Solo

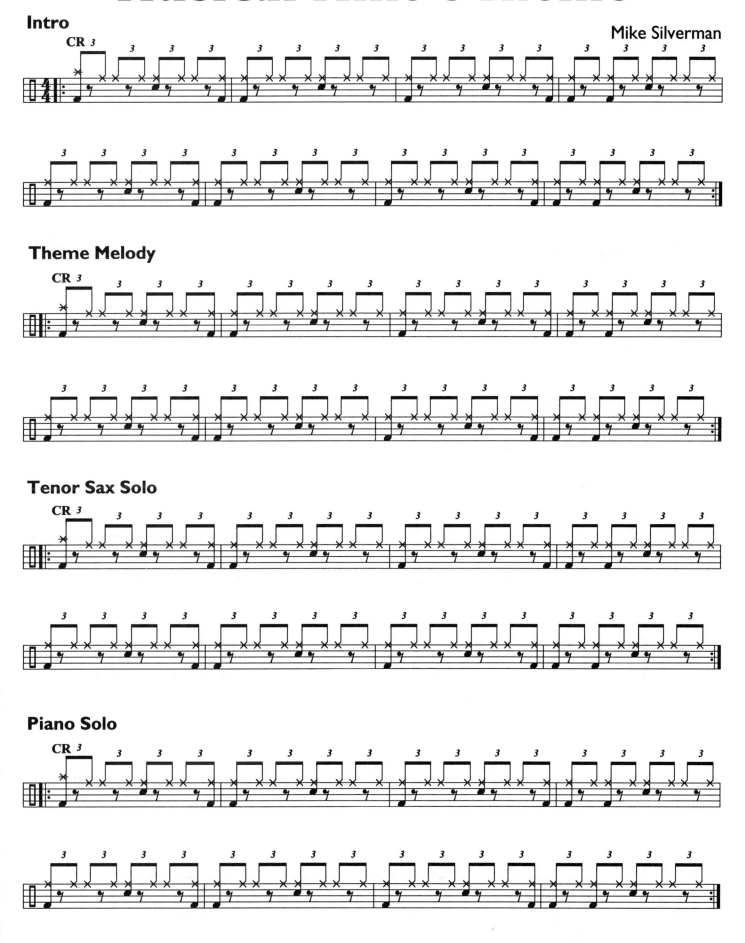

Theme Melody

2nd Tenor Sax Solo

2nd Piano Solo

Theme Melody

Rockin' Rob's Rock Song

Repeat Intro

R L R R L R

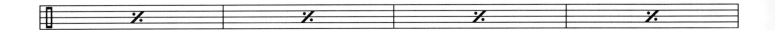

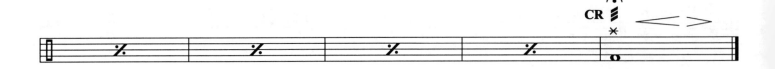

The Drumming Blues

Mike Silverman
Rob Silverman

Muted Trumpet Solo

Organ Solo

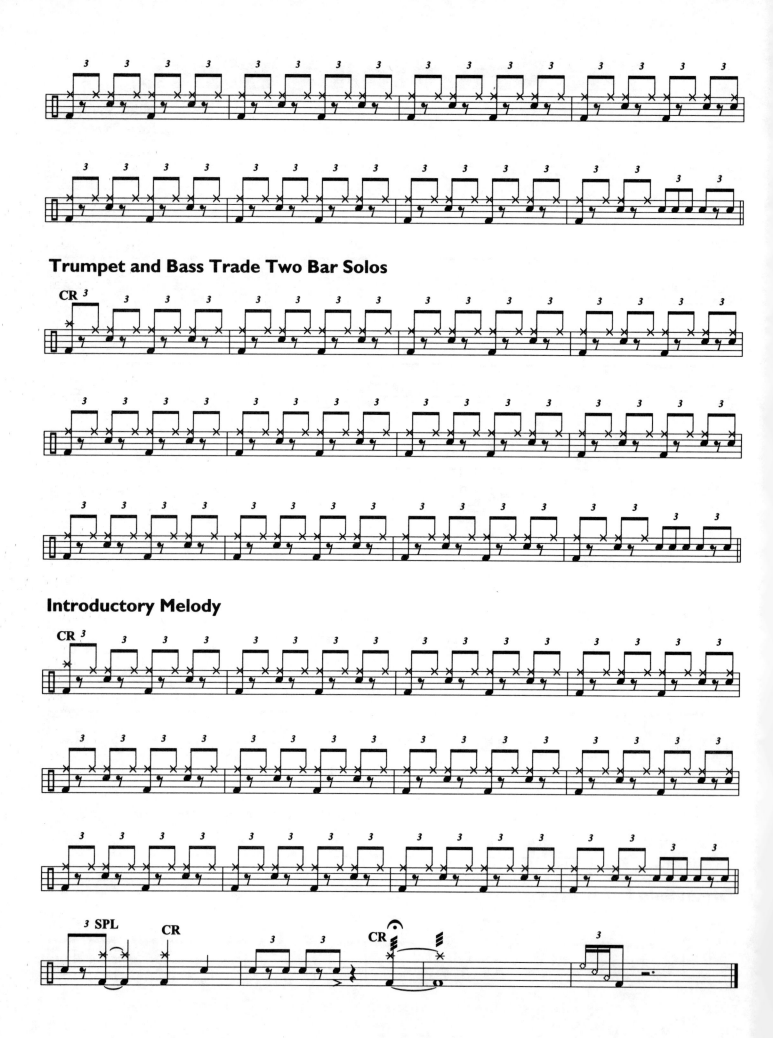

Trumpet and Bass Trade Two Bar Solos

Introductory Melody

One Fine Day

Mike Silverman

Guitar Intro

Main Melody

B Melody

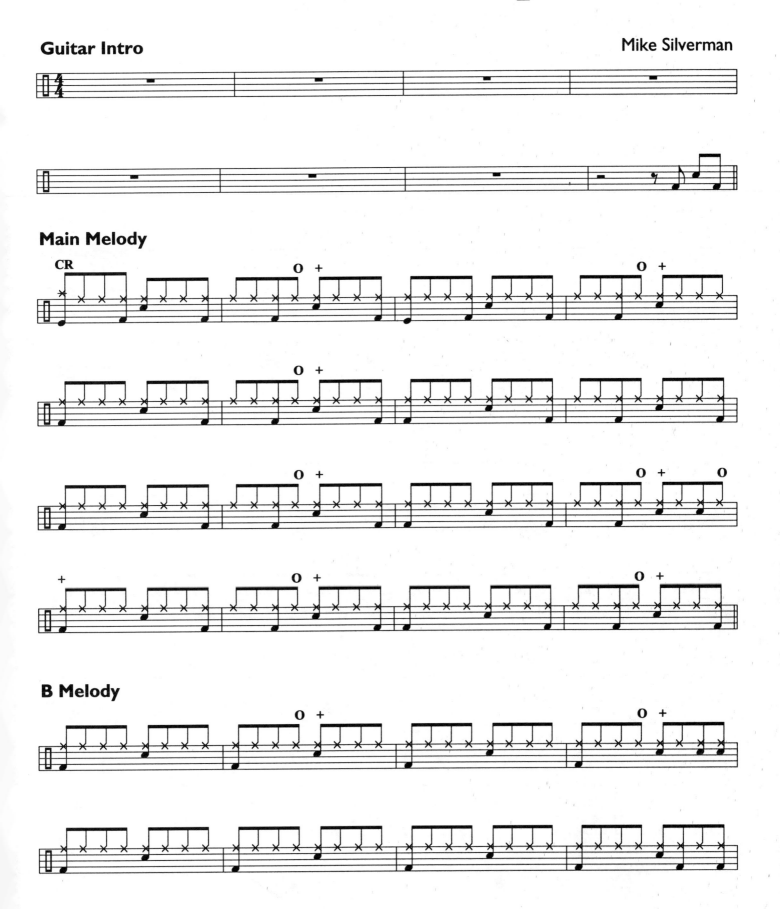

Bridge

Cross stick

Main Melody

101

Glossary of Musical Terms

Time signature. The top number tells you how many beats are in a measure. The bottom number tells you the note value that receives one beat.

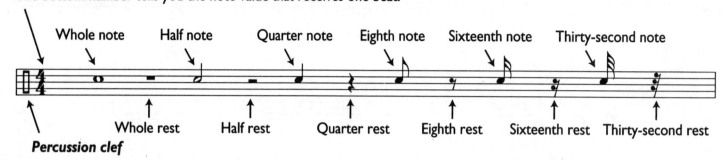

Dynamic marks

ppp	**Pianisissimo**	(extremely soft)
pp	**Pianissimo**	(extremely soft)
p	**Piano**	(soft)
mp	**Mezzo piano**	(moderately soft)
mf	**Mezzo forte**	(medium loud)
f	**Forte**	(loud)
ff	**Fortissimo**	(very loud)
fff	**Fortisissimo**	(extremely loud)

Tempo marks

Slow	**Largo**	(broad, stately)
	Grave	(heavy, dragging)
	Lento	(slow)
	Adagio	(slow, tranquil)
	Andante	(Moving, going along)
	Moderato	(moderate tempo)
	Allegro	(brisk, lively)
Fast	**Presto**	(rapid)
	Tempo di marcia	(march time)
	Vivace	(quick)

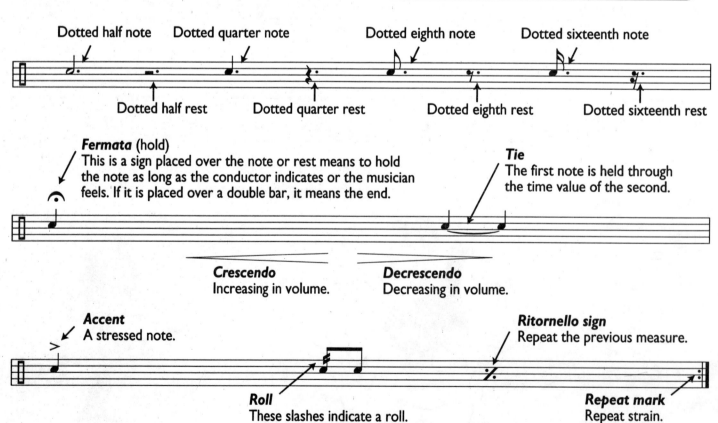

Fermata (hold)
This is a sign placed over the note or rest means to hold the note as long as the conductor indicates or the musician feels. If it is placed over a double bar, it means the end.

Tie
The first note is held through the time value of the second.

Crescendo
Increasing in volume.

Decrescendo
Decreasing in volume.

Accent
A stressed note.

Ritornello sign
Repeat the previous measure.

Roll
These slashes indicate a roll.

Repeat mark
Repeat strain.

More Musical Terms

Cutoff mark
(watch conductor)

D.C. al fine
Repeat from beginning
to fine.

To coda
Go to the coda sign.

Coda sign
Marks the beginning
of the coda.

Sforzando
Strongly accented.

D.C.
Da Capo
Wherever D.C. is found, go back
to the beginning of the piece.

𝄋 **(D.S.)**

Dal segno sign
Wherever the D.S. sign is found,
it means that the section of music
is to be repeated.

D.C. al coda
Go back to the beginning and
play to the coda or "to coda".

(D.C.) 𝄋
This means, go back to the
beginning and play to the sign.

Double bar
The end.

Gradually slow down tempo.
rit.
Ritardando
Meno mosso
Allargando
Rallatando

Gradually speed up tempo.
Accelerando
Piu Mosso
Stringendo

First time . . .
Play first ending

Second time . . .
Skip first measure . . .
Play second ending

1.

2.

(If there are more than two endings, proceed to the next unplayed ending each time through.)

Rudiments

All rudiments should be practiced: *open* (slow) to *closed* (fast) to *open* (slow) and/or at an even moderate tempo.

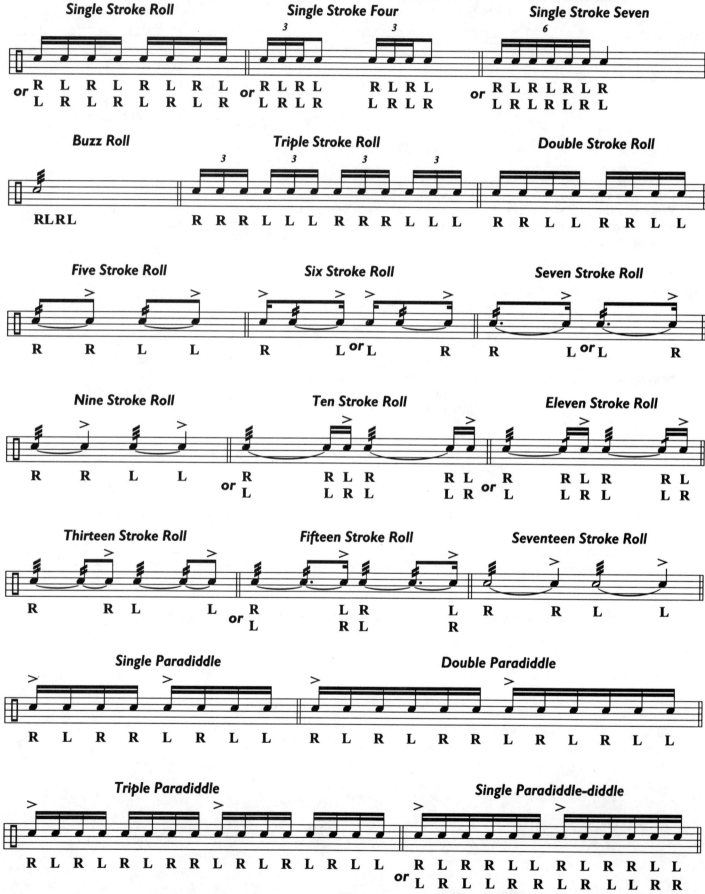

Flams

To play a flam properly, begin by holding your right stick 12 inches above the drum and your left stick 3 inches above the drum. Drop both sticks simultaneously, allowing the left stick to strike the drum just before the right stick. The right stick should fall precisely on the beat.

LR   LR   LR   LR   LR LR LR LR   LR LR LR LR

Now try playing the flam holding your left stick 12 inches above the drum and your right stick 3 inches above the drum.

RL   RL   RL   RL   RL RL RL RL   RL RL RL RL

Now try alternating the sticking. When alternating flams, pay special attention to the lower stick. Make sure it is consistent with each stroke.

LR RL LR RL   RL LR RL LR   LR RL LR RL   LR RL LR RL

Flam Rudiments

Practice each rudiment five times without stopping.

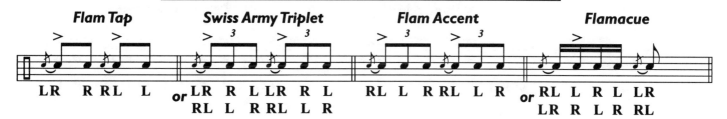

Flam Tap
LR   R RL   L   or

Swiss Army Triplet
LR R L LR R L
RL L R RL L R

Flam Accent
RL L   R RL   L   R   or

Flamacue
RL L R L LR
LR R L R RL

Flam Paradiddle
RL L L R R RL R L L

Single Flammed Mill
LR R L R RL L R L

Pataflafla
LR L R RL RL LR R RL

Flam Drag
LR LL R RL R RL

Flam Paradiddle-diddle
LR L R R L L RL   R L L R R

Inverted Flam Tap
LR   L   RL   R

Drags

The proper way to play a drag is similar to the flam. Hold your right stick 3 inches above the drum and your left stick 6 inches above the drum. The lower stick strikes twice just before the upper stick. The upper stick should strike squarely on the beat. The lower stick provides a broadening effect just barely before the beat. The two grace notes' time value is stolen from the beat immediately preceding the drag.

Left Drag	**Right Drag**	**Alternating**
RRL RRL RRL RRL	LLR LLR LLR LLR	RRL LLR RRL LLR

Drag Rudiments

All rudiments should be practiced: *open* (slow) to *closed* (fast) to *open* (slow) and/or at an even march tempo.

Single Drag Tap   **Double Drag Tap**   **Lesson 25**

LLR   L   RRL   R   LLR LLR   L RRL RRL   R   *or*   LLR   L   R   LLR   L   R
                                                      RRL   R   L   RRL   R   L

Single Dragadiddle   **Drag Paradiddle #1**   **Drag Paradiddle #2**

RRL R R LLR L L   R LLR L R R L RRL R L L   R LLR LLR L R R L RRL RRL R L L

Single Ratamacue   **Double Ratamacue**   **Triple Ratamacue**

LLR L R L RRL R L R   LLR LLR L R L RRL RRL R L R   LLR LLR LLR L R L RRL RRL RRL R L R

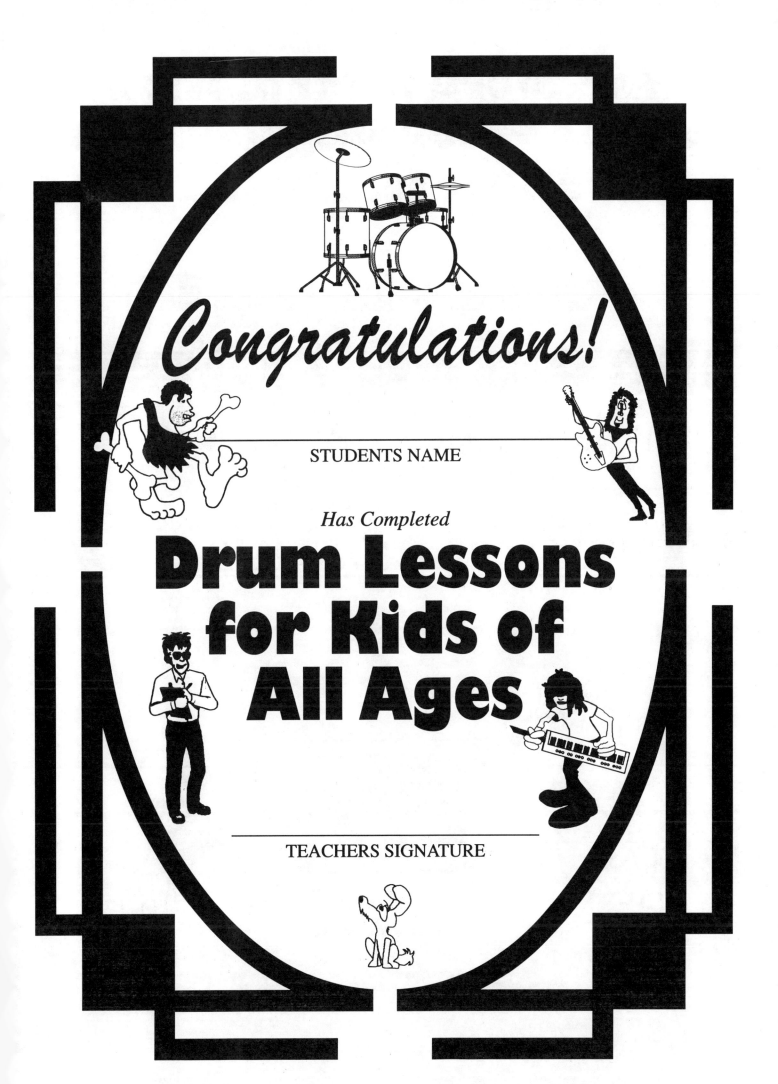

Congratulations!

_____

STUDENTS NAME

Has Completed

Drum Lessons for Kids of All Ages

_____

TEACHERS SIGNATURE

For more information about recordings, clinics and workshops,

check out Rob and Mike's Website at

www.SilvermanMusic.com

Other Books by Rob Silverman

Drumset 101
MB95457BCD

Published by
Mel Bay
Publications, Inc.

Snare Drum 101
MB96672BCD

Drumset for the Twenty-First Century
MB95790BCD

Teachers Notes

Teachers Notes

Teachers Notes